50 FIRST VICTORIES

50 FIRST VICTORIES

NASCAR DRIVERS' BREAKTHROUGH WINS

AL PEARCE AND MIKE HEMBREE

OCTANE
PRESS

Octane Press, Edition 1.0 (softcover), November 2022
Edition 1.0 (hardcover), August 2022
Copyright © 2022 by Al Pearce and Mike Hembree

On the cover:
Main image is Dale Earnhardt Jr.'s first win
at Texas Motor Speedway. *Nigel Kinrade*

Inset cover images:
Dale Earnhardt Sr. *Don Smyle*
Richard Petty. *Dick Conway*
Jimmie Johnson. *David Griffin*
Chase Elliott. *David Griffin*

On the last page:
Authors Al Pearce and Mike Hembree at
Daytona International Speedway. *Jeff Robinson*

ISBN: 978-1-64234-154-6
Hardcover ISBN: 978-1-64234-098-3
ePub ISBN: 978-1-64234-120-1
LCCN: 2022935177

Design by Tom Heffron
Copyedited by Dana Henricks
Proofread by Faith Garcia

octanepress.com

Octane Press is based in Austin, Texas

Printed in the United States

DEDICATION

Dedicated to Leonard Wood and Dale Inman—
brilliant innovators, auto racing legends, and longtime friends

CONTENTS

CONTENTS

CONTENTS

Don't Celebrate Past Midnight

By Kyle Petty

I've been blessed to have been around winners all my life. My grand-dad, Lee, won three NASCAR championships and fifty-four races before injuries forced him to retire in 1963. My dad, Richard, won seven championships and 200 races before he retired in 1992. I was fortunate enough to win eight times, helping my family reach 262 victories. And I have no doubt my young son, Adam, would have become a winner if we hadn't lost him at Loudon in 2000. Those 262 victories, by the way, are more than twice as many as any other family in NASCAR.

Legendary National Football League coach Vince Lombardi once said, "Winning isn't everything, it's the only thing." Bear Bryant, the Hall of Fame football coach at Alabama, had a similar take: "Winning isn't every-thing, but it beats anything that comes in second." And Mia Hamm, the great soccer player at the University of North Carolina and for the United States national team, once said: "The person who said winning isn't every-thing has never won anything."

When I was growing up, the biggest thing at Petty Enterprises wasn't necessarily *racing* itself; it was *getting ready* to race. Dad had this rule about celebrating: no matter where we were or what race we'd just run or whether it was a day race or a night race, his rule was that we didn't celebrate past midnight.

To him, getting to midnight meant we'd accomplished whatever we'd set out to accomplish on *that particular day*. But after midnight we'd better start getting ready for the *next day*. It's like Indiana basketball coach Bobby Knight once said: "The key is not the *will* to win . . . everybody has that. It's the will to *prepare to win* that's important."

Don't get me wrong . . . our family and people at Petty Enterprises were happy to win. We never took it lightly, whether it was a short-track race in small-town America or the Daytona 500 with its international audience. We loved to pile into victory lane together, but we didn't get so excited about the latest victory that we didn't work hard preparing to get the next one.

Many of the fifty drivers in this book are household names not just in NASCAR, but in other disciplines . . . like Mario and A. J. The book includes Hall of Famers with triple-digit victories and others with maybe just one or two. There are drivers you may not have ever heard about but were newsworthy for how they got their first victory.

Two of NASCAR's most experienced beat writers—imagine what they've seen in their ninety-some combined seasons—chronicle how fifty drivers reached the Cup level. Once there, what went into their first major victory? How did they react to their first victory lane? You'll learn things you probably never knew about the sport's greatest drivers. Every first victory has its own backstory, and Mike and Al tell those stories like nobody ever has.

Take it chapter by chapter at your own leisure or devour the whole book over a weekend. Either way, you'll enjoy reading the stories behind these fifty first victories.

CHAPTER 1

Dale Earnhardt

Bristol (TN) Motor Speedway, Apr. 1, 1979

Doug Richert fired up a cigarette in the infield at Bristol Motor Speedway, unaware it would be one of his last smokes. Ever.

Later that afternoon—April 1, 1979 (yes, April Fools' Day), Richert stood in victory lane at Bristol with his fellow crewmen and the driver who had carried them there. Dale Earnhardt had won the Southeastern 500, scoring his first NASCAR Cup victory.

It was no joke, no April Fools' trick. And there stood Richert, eighteen years old and still basically a kid in this big new world of NASCAR, with his cigarette pack torn to pieces.

"In 1979 we won that first race at Bristol, and it was like, 'Whoa,'" Richert remembered. "I quit smoking in victory lane. I told the guys in the shop that when we won for the first time, I'd quit. I tore them up in victory lane at Bristol. Haven't touched one since."

It was cold turkey for Richert but a hot moment for the twenty-seven-year-old Earnhardt, who used Bristol as his platform for turning raw talent into real success. A Carolinas short-track star who had muscled his way into NASCAR's top series, Earnhardt on that Sunday began the journey that would carry him to heights unknown by previous drivers and to riches far beyond the normal reach of a North Carolina mill-hill kid.

Earnhardt won the Cup Rookie of the Year Award that season, grabbed the series championship from older and smarter drivers the next year, and was on his way to seven championships and a type of fan worship that only Richard Petty had experienced.

He became a legend.

Petty won his seventh—and final—championship in 1979. Earnhardt's title the next year was the first of his seven. The Earnhardt era had barely begun. He improved quickly, evolving from the fender banging of late model stock racing to the much longer and more complicated racing demanded by Cup events. He kept his super-aggressive driving form but factored in the new dynamics needed to score at stock car racing's highest level.

"It's like he'd been there forever," said Richert, who was promoted from mechanic to crew chief for the 1980 season after veteran crew chief Jake Elder left the Rod Osterlund–owned team. "It was really kind of amazing how well it flowed along and how competitive he was." It was Elder, by the way, who famously offered Earnhardt some overly colorful advice in Bristol's victory lane: "Stick with me, boy, and we'll have diamonds big as horse turds."

Dale Earnhardt's last win came in spectacular fashion. He raced from eighteenth place to first in the closing laps at Talladega Superspeedway, October 15, 2000.

Elder, who had a reputation for jumping suddenly from one team to another, was with Earnhardt long enough to pass along some of the encyclopedic knowledge he had gained from years in the sport. "I remember Jake talking to him about running off the top of the corner and don't overdrive and things like that," Richert said. "I remember Dale complaining somewhere about how the car was pushing out of Turn Four. Jake got on the radio and said, 'Dale, I can do a lot of things, but I can't stop the wind from blowing.'"

Earnhardt led 163 of the 500 laps in the Bristol win and held off veteran Bobby Allison by three seconds at the checkered. "This is a bigger thrill than my first-ever racing victory," he said in the middle of a

Dale Earnhardt communicates with his pit crew at Bristol Motor Speedway. *DICK CONWAY*

wild Bristol celebration. "This was a win in the big leagues, against the top-caliber drivers. It wasn't some dirt track back at home."

Earnhardt didn't win again in the 1979 season, but he performed well enough to bring in enough cash to buy a house on Lake Norman near Charlotte. He was on his way.

"I think about how fast things have changed, and it scares me a little," he said later that season. "But I will take it. I am always in a hurry. There is always something else to do. That hasn't changed. I don't want to go back to where I was, but I don't ever want to forget where I came from, either."

And he didn't. Until his final race, when he was killed in a last-lap crash in the 2001 Daytona 500, Earnhardt retained a strong connection to a rabid fan base. He had fought his way from the Kannapolis, North Carolina, mill village and from dead-end jobs to become one of the most successful—and richest—race car drivers in the world. Blue-collar fans, traditionally the heart of NASCAR, loved him for his past and the fact

A rugged
mustache
was a Dale
Earnhardt
trademark for
most of his
career.
DICK CONWAY

that he didn't shed his Carolina roots. He was one of them. Just much wealthier.

Earnhardt had been bitten by the racing bug on that very mill hill. His father, Ralph, was a short-track racing star, and Dale idolized him. The two worked on Ralph's cars in the small garage behind the modest Earnhardt home. Although Dale missed many of his father's races, he could walk into the garage early the next morning and figure out how Ralph had done based on the amount of dirt and mud on the car. If the front end of the car was relatively clean, that meant his father had led most of the night and probably had won.

Ralph died of a heart attack in 1973 at the age of forty-five. His son was left to race alone.

"Dale was really a self-made guy," said NASCAR historian Buz McKim. "He started out with nothing. Ralph had nothing to pass on to him. Dale made it on his own with little education but a lot of determination and talent. He'll be the guy looked on forever as the working man's man."

Some say Earnhardt is the best NASCAR driver of all time. He joined Richard Petty, Junior Johnson, Bill France Sr., and Bill France Jr. in the first NASCAR Hall of Fame class.

After winning a seventh championship to tie Petty in titles, Earnhardt offered this analysis of his standing: "I'll never be King Richard, not even King Dale. There's only one king in NASCAR, and that's Richard Petty."

Dale Earnhardt owned a Chevrolet dealership in Newton, North Carolina. He got a new pickup truck from the dealership a couple of times a year, swapping the old one, and there was a waiting list of people ready to buy the trucks he had driven.

But Dale Earnhardt carved his own trail to greatness, and much of racing fandom was along for the ride.

"To me, he was iconic, before his time," said long-time NASCAR promoter Ken Clapp. "He stayed that way 'til the day he died. He was our Babe Ruth."

CHAPTER 2

Richard Petty

Southern States (NC) Fairgrounds, Feb. 28, 1960

Lee Petty already had forty-eight NASCAR Cup Series victories by the time his son Richard got his first. It came on February 28, 1960, at the half-mile dirt Southern States Fairgrounds track near Charlotte, North Carolina. The season's sixth race was a two-hundred-lap, one-hundred-miler a week after Junior Johnson won the Daytona 500 over Bobby Johns.

The first of Richard's two hundred victories came later than expected. Indeed, he was flagged the winner of a 1959 race at Lakewood Speedway near Atlanta, Georgia, but second-place Lee successfully protested and got the results reversed. It was Richard's seventeenth Cup start and second place was fine by him.

The race was a "Sweepstakes" open to both convertibles and sedans. Richard drove a 1959 Oldsmobile convertible, his father a 1959 Plymouth sedan. After the race, Lee argued strenuously that he was first and Richard was second. Their finishing order, he insisted, was backward. As was so often the case, money was involved.

The Lakewood entry included a $250 bonus if the winner drove a convertible like Richard's 1959 Oldsmobile. It also offered a $450 bonus if the winner drove a 1959 current-year model like Lee's No. 42

The span between Richard Petty's first win and his 200th (and last) stretched across twenty-five years. *Bill Niven / BRH Racing Archives*

Plymouth. Lee the businessman realized that Petty Enterprises would make more money if he won. His bonus would beat Richard's bonus by $200, serious money at the time. Lee didn't hesitate to protest for the extra money.

Richard knew better than to complain. "Second was the best I'd ever run, so I was tickled," Richard said many years later. "I was out of the car jumping around 'cause I'd just won for the first time. Then, somebody came over and said Daddy had protested. Later, he explained that we'd make more money with him winning, and we needed every little bit we could get.

"Really . . . it didn't matter that much to me. I was just a twenty-one-year-old kid happy to be there. All I cared about was that we had enough cars and money so I could keep racing. It didn't make that much difference as long as the company came out ahead. In the end, I think the scorers got it right."

The next day, in the *Atlanta Constitution*, a sportswriter quoted Lee as saying, "Either way you look at it, we are one-two. But I won the race. He's my boy and I would love to see him win. But when he does, I want him to earn it. I would have protested my mother if I needed to."

A year before Lakewood, in July 1958, the Pettys raced together in Toronto, Canada. The first of Richard's record 1,184 starts also was the first of his

Across the years, Richard Petty's No. 43 racer became one of the most famous cars in the history of motorsports. How famous? The Smithsonian has one.

record 984 losses . . . and Lee was again in the middle of things. Two weeks after turning twenty-one, Richard qualified seventh for the

A cowboy hat and sunglasses have defined Richard Petty's fashion sense for decades.
DICK CONWAY

one-hundred-lap race in the No. 142 Oldsmobile. He barely reached halfway before crashing out and finishing seventeenth. But there's more to it than just another racing accident.

The flagman that day was NASCAR official Ross Kennedy. He had a clear view of the third-mile track and blamed Lee for wrecking Richard. "Richard was all over the track," Kennedy once told a journalist. "Lee was leading, and he came around and there was Richard, in the way. WHOOMP! That was the end for Richard." (Clearly, the elder Petty took no prisoners, not even his son.)

"Everything was Daddy's deal about where we raced and when," Richard explained when asked about his schedule. "He said we were going to Canada, so we loaded up and went to Canada." As usual, Richard knew not to complain about the crash: "It wasn't much of a start for me," Richard told reporters afterward, "but Daddy won, so it was good for the Pettys."

The future superstar made eight more starts in 1958 and twenty-one more in his Rookie of the Year season of 1959. By the time he went full-schedule racing in 1960, he already had six top fives and ten top tens. Clearly, the potential was there, but not the results.

That potential finally bloomed in February of 1960 at Charlotte. At twenty-two and still learning, Richard qualified seventh among twenty-one entrants in what became a controversial and confusing race. Never mind questions about lap leaders, lead changes, contact, and (perhaps) intentional teamwork.

One version has No. 2 qualifier Rex White leading much of the race with Richard close behind the future Hall of Famer. Richard was second at lap 182 when (according to Richard) White hit a huge hole in Turn One and lost momentum. Richard passed cleanly and drove

The Pettys' NASCAR experience spread to four generations. Richard followed Lee. Richard's son, Kyle, also raced and won, and Adam, Kyle's son, seemed destined to join the family winning list before he lost his life in an accident at New Hampshire Motor Speedway.

Richard Petty prepares for one of his 1,184 Cup Series starts. *Dick Conway*

off toward his first career victory. Two leaders and one lead change; nothing unusual about that.

Another version is that Lee Petty, relief driving for Doug Yates, simply knocked White aside to make Richard's pass easier. It's unclear from accounts whether White and Lee had been together all day or whether White was so dominant that Lee had to wait until the end to move him aside using another man's car.

"Honestly, I don't remember much about that race," Richard said recently. "It was a long time ago. I do remember the track was unbearably rough, but not much else about what went on. There were potholes and bumps and ruts all over the place. Rex got into one of them and I went by him. I got through the rough spots better than he did. Only about seven of us were running at the end."

White, now ninety-three, remembers Lee knocking him aside late, ruining his chance of winning. "We'll never know if I could have won," he said several years ago. "But I certainly was in contention until Lee hit me. As much as I raced with Richard through the years, I never had any confrontation or disagreement with him. He didn't do a thing to me that afternoon. But I didn't get along with Lee, not one bit. And I wasn't the only one. No, sir."

When asked about the incident later, Lee Petty told a *Charlotte Observer* reporter: "I didn't hurt Richard's chances."

Hmmm?

CHAPTER 3

Jeff Gordon

Charlotte (NC) Motor Speedway, May 29, 1994

I t's impossible to chronicle the fullness of NASCAR's history without a few words about Jeff Gordon. Maybe a chapter in a book. Or even a few chapters. Perhaps a book all to itself. Even a full shelf of books about one of racing's most accomplished drivers. After all, the driver once referred to as "Wonderboy" helped change the sport for all time.

Gordon's career stretched a quarter century and produced some of the Cup Series's most enduring and endearing moments. It's likely that only a few competitors will ever be considered in his class, maybe a half dozen whose influence helped mold the sport into what we have today.

Jeffrey Michael Gordon stands amidst them.

From California by way of Indiana, the Hall of Famer came to stock cars after success on ESPN's Thursday Night Thunder in the mid- to late-1980s. Those telecasts gave many Americans their first look at USAC's Sprint Car, Midget, and Silver Crown stars, and Gordon certainly was among them. He was young, handsome, personable, and articulate, a rock star/teen idol clearly headed for bigger and better things.

At first, NASCAR wasn't prominent on his radar. He honed his skills and built his reputation in open-wheel, so IndyCar and the Indy 500 seemed logical destinations. But he fell into the clutches of

Jeff Gordon,
young, fast,
and popular,
revolutionized
NASCAR in
the 1990s.
David Griffin

NASCAR because he and his family couldn't marshal the funds to buy a competitive IndyCar ride. History has recorded open-wheel's loss as stock car's gain.

He took a friend's advice and attended the Buck Baker Driving School at the North Carolina Speedway at Rockingham. There, performing well and blessed by fate, he met stock car devotees who introduced him to mechanics who introduced him to team reps who introduced him to team owners. A couple of successful Xfinity Series seasons with owner Bill Davis led to an incomparable career in Cup with owner Rick Hendrick. For most of those years, crew chief Ray Evernham guided the No. 24 program to unprecedented heights.

From a one-off in 1992 at age twenty until his retirement at age forty-four in 2016, Gordon made 805 Cup starts, won eighty-one poles and ninety-three races, had twenty-one top-ten points seasons, hoisted four championship trophies, and won almost every significant race at least once. He's in every meaningful motorsports hall of fame and is generally considered the first in the "new wave" of drivers who were as socially and commercially savvy in the boardroom as they were talented behind the wheel.

Richard Petty and David Pearson had brought NASCAR to the country's attention in the 1960s and 1970s. Darrell Waltrip and Dale Earnhardt had led the way in the 1980s and 1990s. Gordon dominated throughout the 1990s and into the new century. A litany of well-backed, well-connected, aggressive young kids eventually moved into Gordon's turf, marking the end of another era.

The first of his ninety-three victories—that's third all-time behind Petty's 200 and Pearson's 105—came in the 1994 Coca-Cola 600 at Charlotte Motor Speedway (CMS). In their forty previous starts, Gordon and Evernham had finished top five in nine races and top ten in five more, showing the potential that would soon blossom. They had been second to Earnhardt in the 1993 Coca-Cola 600 and fifth in that season's fall race at CMS, and had two Xfinity victories there, both from the pole. Plus, they had started on pole for two of their three Cup races at the 1.5-mile track. Clearly, Charlotte was theirs for the taking.

Rusty Wallace and Geoffrey Bodine dominated the four-hundred-lapper, Wallace leading 197 laps and Bodine 101. But both made late-race pit stops for four tires and fuel. Evernham waited as long as possible, leaving his Chevrolet Lumina out until everyone else

Most fans remember Earnhardt as NASCAR's dominant figure during the eight years he and Gordon were rivals. But between 1993 and 2000 Gordon had more than twice as many victories and two more championships. Each beat the other four times in the final standings.

Jeff Gordon leads Hendrick Motorsports teammate Jimmie Johnson.
DAVID GRIFFIN

had stopped. Knowing they had only one chance, Evernham called for a splash of fuel and only right-side tires. The two-tire stop for 8.65 seconds got Gordon back out ahead of Wallace, whose four-tire stop had taken about sixteen seconds. Gordon rode that strategy to his breakthrough victory over Wallace by almost four seconds.

"It wasn't really a gamble," Evernham said at the time, almost overcome by the emotion of his first victory. "We really didn't have any choice; sometimes you've just gotta go for it. If you can't beat 'em one way, you have to beat 'em another. I just can't believe this."

Gordon concurred: "Two was the absolute best decision," he said as tears covered his cheeks. "We didn't need a full fuel load, and the two rights actually balanced the car and kept me fast. We weren't about to beat Rusty otherwise. Nobody was; he was that good all night. But sometimes the fastest car doesn't win."

Later, when the impact of the moment cleared, Evernham explained his strategy. "We could have changed two or four or done a gas-and-go," he said. "It made my decision easier when Rusty and Geoffrey took four ahead of us. We figured the time we'd save with a two-tire stop would be worth it in the long run. Hey . . . I'll always bet on my guy when he's leading with ten laps left."

Gordon's on-track fame led to several notable off-track opportunities. He was among the first athletes to host *Saturday Night Live* and was a popular and well-received repeat guest on the morning show co-hosted by Regis Philbin and Kelly Ripa. He also appeared on (among others) the movie *Taxi*, David Letterman, Jay Leno, *The Today Show*, Jimmy Kimmel, Ellen DeGeneres, *60 Minutes*, Rachael Ray, and Jimmy Fallon.

The winning strategy left Wallace's crew chief second-guessing his four-tire call. "We never dreamed they would do what they did," Buddy Parrott said of the Rainbow Warriors. "We figured we'd be racing (Bodine) for the win, not Gordon. It was a chancy move for them to take just two because I never thought it would work. Looking back, we should have taken two tires and won by a ton. We really had everybody beat bad that night."

Gordon's second career win came later that year, in the inaugural Brickyard 400 at Indianapolis Motor Speedway. He won ten, ten, and thirteen races in 1996, 1997, and 1998, and was winless only three times in his twenty-three full seasons. He won the 600 again in 1997 and 1998, and the Brickyard 400 again in 1998, 2001, 2004, and 2014. He was an overwhelming choice—although not unanimously—for the 2019 NASCAR Hall of Fame class.

CHAPTER 4

Jim Roper

Charlotte (NC) Speedway, June 19, 1949

It's funny how Jim Roper won the first race in what is now the NASCAR Cup Series.

It's funny because, without the funnies, Roper would never have known about organizer Bill France Sr.'s decision to schedule the first race in his new stock car series at the now-defunct Charlotte Speedway, a three-quarter-mile dirt track near what is now the Charlotte, North Carolina, airport.

The two-hundred-lap race was run June 19, 1949, and it was an audacious event. France took a chance that people interested in automobile racing would jump at the idea of watching cars fresh from showroom floors race in close quarters. This new division, called Strictly Stock by France, would be a dramatic departure from the Modified and "jalopy" racing fans had grown accustomed to.

In part because of the newness of the event (and in part because of France's promotional genius), the race drew widespread interest. In this case, "widespread" included the state of Kansas, where sometimes racer Jim Roper lived. The race was mentioned in a newspaper comic strip (sometimes called "the funnies") penned by Zack Mosley, and Roper happened to see it in a local paper.

Fast cars? $2,000 to win? A chance to rip off fast laps in a brand new car? Roper was in.

Roper drove a showroom-new Lincoln from Kansas to North Carolina and entered the race—in that car. He didn't really know what to expect, but he didn't lack confidence. "Man, the only idea I ever had was to win," he said in a 1998 interview.

Pumped by France's promotional skills and announcements by local news media outlets, it was clear early race morning that the event would be a roaring success. Spectators parked their cars miles away and walked to the track, which had been in operation about a year and had hosted Modified racing.

The first Strictly Stock race, won by Roper, included a woman in the field. Sara Christian qualified thirteenth and finished fourteenth, her Ford a victim of overheating.

"There were fans here at 6:00 a.m. that day," said David Allison, son of Carl Allison, the property's owner. "Cars were parked as far as four miles away. We had people climbing trees to see. Daddy would crank up a chainsaw and go over there. He wouldn't actually cut the trees down, but they would come out of them anyway."

By race time, more than ten thousand people—some estimates put the crowd number at over twenty thousand, likely an exaggeration—had jammed into the track. They saw action that has been described as barely controlled mayhem as the heavy cars banged around a dusty surface pockmarked by holes. And they saw drivers who would become stars of the fledgling sport—Lee Petty, Tim Flock, Fonty Flock, Curtis Turner, Buck Baker, Jack Smith, and Herb Thomas.

The winner, though, would be Chris "Jim" Roper (he used "Jim" as a racing name), a man unknown to virtually everyone else at the track that day. He led forty-seven laps in the second half of the race, but North Carolina driver Glenn Dunaway charged to the front late and took the checkered flag first. Roper was a distant second, but that would change.

The race was a dusty marathon. Only eleven of the thirty-three starters finished as overheating problems parked many entries. And the roughness of the track caused some drivers to leave the race with broken wheels.

Among the spectators that day was Ned Jarrett, who would become a NASCAR star himself in the next decade.

"I was standing next to the fence at the start-finish line," he said. "I thought that was the place to be. All of a sudden, a car came down through there and a fan blade flew off and stuck in the wooden post right where I was leaning. I quickly figured out that was not the place to be."

"Overheating" was listed as the reason seven of the race's thirty-three cars failed to finish. Roper's winning car also overheated near the end of the race, but he was able to nurse the car home by reducing his speed.

While Dunaway celebrated, NASCAR officials began a post-race check of his winning Ford. Soon, word came that he had been disqualified because the rear end of his car, a converted moonshine hauler, had been strengthened to support loads of illegal liquor. Such modifications didn't fit NASCAR rules.

Roper was declared the winner but not before the engine in his Lincoln was torn down for inspection. Fortunately for Roper, a local Ford dealership gave him a new engine. It was installed in the car, and Roper drove home in the Cup Series's first winning vehicle.

"It was a very controversial race," Roper remembered years later. "I think it was one of the things that helped make NASCAR, due to the controversy. It was more or less competitive, too."

Not surprisingly, Dunaway and car owner Hubert Westmoreland were not pleased by NASCAR's decision. Westmoreland said NASCAR approved his car prior to the race. He eventually sued, but a court ruled that NASCAR controlled the rules of its races, setting a key precedent for France.

It was the first major controversy for NASCAR's new series, but it certainly would not be the last. "I think that was the worst injustice that I ever saw NASCAR do anybody," said driver Jack Smith, who finished thirteenth that day.

Roper drove in only one other NASCAR race, finishing fifteenth at Occoneechee Speedway in Hillsborough, North Carolina, later that season.

He eventually moved from Halstead, Kansas, to Kaufman, Texas, where he operated a horse farm for most of the rest of his life. He died in 2000.

CHAPTER 5

Bobby Allison

Oxford Plains (ME) Speedway, July 12, 1966

It's ironic that Bobby Allison made his name by winning NASCAR Cup Series races on long, fast, high-banked superspeedways in the South. Ironic, because the first of his eighty-four career victories came on a tiny, rough-and-tumble, backwoods bullring in central Maine— about as far from his south Florida and Alabama roots as possible.

Before those victories at Daytona Beach and Charlotte, there was Oxford Plains. Before he conquered Dover and Talladega, there was Oxford Plains. And before he won the 1983 Cup Series title, entered the NASCAR Hall of Fame in 2011, and won seven Most Popular Driver Awards, there was Oxford Plains.

And before losing two sons to racing and almost losing his own life to racing, there was Oxford Plains Speedway, a third-mile chunk of antiquity that's still going strong.

As with so many young and ambitious racers of that time, Allison scoring his first Cup victory barely made headlines outside the home area of the speedway. The Oxford 300 in July of 1966 was the third stop on NASCAR's annual Northern swing that included stops in Manassas, Virginia, followed by races at Bridgehampton, New York, and Oxford, then Fonda and Islip in New York.

Bobby Allison raced from the smallest track to the biggest superspeedways and won virtually everywhere.
DAVID GRIFFIN

Allison, twenty-eight and relatively inexperienced, began on pole but finished a transmission-related fifteenth at Manassas on July 7. Three nights later he started fifteenth and finished an engine-related twenty-third on the Bridgehampton Road Course. The first of his eighty-four victories came at Oxford on July 12, when he started on pole and led most of the three hundred laps. There was little drama during the race, but just getting there was an adventure.

Allison remembers it well. "My oil pan at Bridgehampton wasn't right, so I lost oil pressure whenever I made a right-hand turn," he said. "It took only a couple of rights to burn the rod bearings. But I was so much better than the field-fillers that I could pit, work on the engine, replace some parts, and go back out. I finished the race, but was out of spare parts. I didn't have anything in the hauler for the next race."

Undeterred, Allison and crewman Chuck Looney stopped at a Chevrolet dealership on their way to Maine. The parts department didn't have the new Corvette short-block assembly that Allison needed, but $250 got him a used block, new rods, and new bearings. Later that day he rented a small workspace at a racer-friendly Chevy dealership close to Oxford Plains. They worked all night putting the refreshed engine in their 1965 Chevelle.

In his pre-NASCAR days Allison briefly went by "Bob Sunderman" so his parents in south Florida wouldn't know he was racing.

"That's how we sometimes had to do things," Allison said, then added, "at least *some of us* had to do that. But we wouldn't have made that race if we hadn't. After some practice laps, I knew the car would be good, and it was. [He led the final 238 laps, lapping the field.] And let me tell you: winning in Cup was everything I'd dreamed it would be. I'd always known I could

Bobby Allison roared in from Alabama to challenge Richard Petty for NASCAR dominance. *Dick Conway*

do it because I'd beaten up on some pretty big Modified names getting to Cup. Oxford was a big, big deal for me. I celebrated by going to bed."

Allison and Looney finished the tour with a crash-related twenty-seventh at Fonda, then won again two days later at Islip. He got his third career victory a month later by starting on pole and winning easily at Beltsville, Maryland. For the most part, the rest of his NASCAR successes were far more newsworthy. They included six victories each at Daytona Beach, Charlotte, and Riverside, five at Darlington, and four at his home track at Talladega.

His first superspeedway victory—his eighth overall—came for Holman-Moody Racing in October of 1967 at Rockingham, North Carolina. There was a five-week stretch in the summer of 1971 when he won on consecutive weekends at Charlotte, Dover, Michigan, Riverside,

Much of Bobby Allison's success was tied to the fact that he knew the intricate nature of race cars from bumper to bumper.
DICK CONWAY

Bobby Allison
and his wife,
Judy, celebrate
in victory lane.
Dick Conway

and Houston. He won ten races each in 1971 and 1972, and won at least once a year for twenty of his twenty-five Cup seasons. Sadly, Allison's career-ending crash at Pocono in the summer of 1988 erased all memory of his one-two finish with Davey, his elder son, in the Daytona 500 earlier that season.

"I've got all kinds of proof that Davey was second, but I can't tell you anything about the race," he said. "I've seen pictures of me and him pouring beer on each other [in victory lane]. I've watched the television tapes and I've read all about it. It's funny how I remember things that happened *around* that day, but nothing about the race itself. I really, really wish I did."

It can be argued that no family in American sports endured as many excruciating losses as the Allisons. He and his wife, Judy, lost one son, twenty-seven-year-old Clifford, in an August 1992 Xfinity practice session in Michigan. They lost their other son, thirty-two-year-old Davey, in a July 1993 aviation accident in Alabama. Bobby's career ended at age fifty in a first-lap accident in June of 1988 at Pocono. He almost died from head and torso injuries that required multiple surgeries, 108 hospital days, and lengthy rehabilitation.

Allison insists he won eighty-five races, but NASCAR says it's eighty-four. He was never credited with his 1971 Grand American (GA) victory in a Mustang at Bowman Gray Stadium, even though the career record of driver Tiny Lund includes two GA victories that same year.

Despite the tragedies, he still embraces the sport. "It has been good to me in a lot of ways," Allison once told journalist Don Coble. "It's been very unfortunate in others. The way I look at it, life, not racing, has presented me with some difficult times. I don't think there's anything wrong with racing. My feeling about life and death is this: life is a gift and death can come at any time. You can't do anything about it."

Despite everything, Allison has never questioned his faith. "I don't get angry because Jesus Christ is my savior," he says when asked what keeps him strong. "When Clifford died, I asked my mother how she did it. How did she hold up after losing five of her own [thirteen] children, including two babies and a teenager? She said something that really, really helped me. She said, 'I just gave them back to God.' And that's what Judy and I did with our boys.

"Now, how wonderful is that?"

CHAPTER 6

Mario Andretti

Daytona (FL) International Speedway, Feb. 16, 1967

M ario Andretti had no significant interest in becoming a stock car racer. His eyes were on the big prizes of open-wheel racing: the Indianapolis 500, IndyCar championships, and Formula 1 glory.

Nevertheless, he looked upon Richard Petty, David Pearson, and other stars of NASCAR as heroes, as a big part of the family of racers who drove to the limit, and often beyond. He wanted to race them and know the feeling of driving a fast car at the front of a pack at Daytona, which was emerging as a racing capital in the mid-1960s as Andretti's career was accelerating.

After a disappointing run in a Smokey Yunick–prepared Chevrolet in the 1966 Daytona 500, Andretti called on his partners at Ford Motor Co. for a ride in the 1967 500, and Ford paired Andretti with the Holman-Moody team, a NASCAR giant of the period. However, even for a driver of Andretti's immense talents, taking on the challenge of high-speed Daytona against drivers with years of stock car experience was daunting.

On day one, as teams assembled on the Atlantic coast for a week of practicing, qualifying, and racing, the challenge became clear. Although Andretti had the Ford stamp of approval, he didn't have Ford's golden

Mario Andretti, an
international racing
superstar, dropped in on
NASCAR and won the
Daytona 500.
DICK CONWAY

ticket. That belonged to Fred Lorenzen, who had become Fast Freddy, a star of the stock car crowd's biggest tracks and, with Hollywood good looks, a popular driver. It was assumed that Lorenzen, already twenty-three times a winner in NASCAR, would have the best equipment Ford could provide in his search for a second Daytona 500 victory.

The race's short history—the first 500 was in 1959—leaned toward the stock car grinders, men who could rub fenders for hours and come out the other side with the checkered flag in sight. The 500's trophy, quickly becoming one of the most sought after pieces of hardware in the sport, had gone to stock car blue bloods like Richard Petty, Lee Petty, Junior Johnson, and Fireball Roberts. And here through the infield tunnel arrived Mario Andretti, loaded for bear.

"Daytona was the star of the show for NASCAR," Andretti said. "With the qualifying procedure and then the qualifying races and the 500, it was unique. We were there for a week. NASCAR was trying to emulate Indianapolis, to make it not just a race but an event. There's no question that it was already the jewel of NASCAR racing."

Andretti's No. 11 Ford was tooled by Jake Elder, at thirty years old already a top NASCAR mechanic. And it showed. "The car unloaded pretty good," Andretti said. "The handling was pretty balanced. I could tell it was a good car. But I wasn't getting the speed. I was running at 6,800 revs. I was talking to Donnie Allison just casually, and I asked him, 'What revs should I be running?' He said at least 7,200.

"So I wondered what some of the other Ford guys were running. I asked a Ford guy if I could see the dyno sheets from the engines they had brought down, and he said they were all within four or five horsepower. They all had name tags on them—Lorenzen, Foyt, some of the others. Mine was there. So I took one of the tags off and swapped it with another. He said, 'You can't do that.' I said, 'The engines are all within four or five horsepower, why not?' He just answered my question."

In 2006, Andretti received the highest honor bestowed by his native Italy, the Commendatore dell'Ordine al Merito della Repubblica Italiana, or Commendatore for short. The Italian government said the award was in recognition of his public service, accomplishments as a driver, and enduring commitment to his Italian heritage.

After discussions with team owner John Holman, an engine built by future NASCAR Hall of Famer Waddell Wilson was dropped into Andretti's car. That made the difference. Andretti was suddenly a contender. "Waddell Wilson deserves the credit," Andretti said. "He built me a strong engine. Now it was up to me to keep from crashing."

Andretti used a soft anti-roll bar that kept the rear of the car loose. He drove low into the turns and then drifted high exiting, a style different from the NASCAR regulars. "I knew I had to try to lead because the car was loose," he said. "I think the other guys figured I was going to crash."

But Andretti took control of the race late, and he and Lorenzen were one-two in the closing miles. They pitted at the same time, and Lorenzen's crew returned him to the track—and into the lead—while Andretti's team jacked up his car and added spring rubbers. "They held me up on purpose because Freddy was the team guy," Andretti said. "But I chased him down and got in front, but I couldn't shake him. We were coming up on the lapped car of Tiny Lund. He pulled to the middle of the track and motioned for me to go to the outside. I pulled right up behind him and shot to the left, almost into the grass. That confused Freddy, I think. I think he backed out. By the time I came out on the other side, I could hardly see him."

Andretti won the Formula 1 championship, a dream swirling in his head since his early childhood, in 1978, scoring six wins across the globe and becoming only the second American to win the world title.

A caution flew with two laps to go, and Andretti had won NASCAR's biggest race.

"It was a most satisfying race for me," he said. "Holman-Moody gave me a great car. Freddy was the top guy. From Ford's standpoint, I could understand it. I was not a regular. But for me to be on a track and be competing with Richard Petty and David Pearson . . . I looked up to those guys. They were my heroes. I figure I'm in that arena with the top drivers NASCAR has to offer, and I'm competitive with them. These are the moments that stay with you forever."

The Daytona 500 trophy has an honored spot in the dazzling array of victory hardware Andretti has on display in his Nazareth, Pennsylvania, home. He raced in NASCAR thirteen other times between 1966 and 1969 but didn't challenge for other wins.

He got NASCAR's big one. There were other hills to climb.

CHAPTER 7

Kyle Larson

Michigan International Speedway, Aug. 28, 2016

Second place is not why Kyle Larson came to NASCAR Cup racing. His early results, however, might have hinted otherwise.

A short-track terror seemingly a lock for success in the major leagues, Larson lagged behind his reputation when he arrived in bigger stock cars. Seconds, thirds, and other top fives were easy to notch; first place was a mystery that he could touch but not quite grasp.

The road to that reality was longer than most expected.

"I had all those seconds and some other finishes that were really close to wins, and you never know if you're going to get it," Larson said. "But I did have confidence that someday we would. It took me almost three seasons to win. A long time. I knew we could do it. We were in contention a lot."

The magic came together August 28, 2016, at Michigan International Speedway (MIS), a track where Larson had had two top-ten runs. Entering the Michigan race, he had logged seven top-ten finishes for the season without winning. Then everything clicked. He led forty-one of two hundred laps (including the last ten) and was a relative calendar page in front of the opposition at the finish, beating Chase Elliott to the finish line by 1.47 seconds. Brad Keselowski was third.

A dirt-track kingpin, Kyle Larson broke into the Cup winners circle in 2016 at Michigan.
DAVID GRIFFIN

The promise had become reality.

"A lot of times when I was leading races I feel like we'd also have a late-race caution and I'd get beat," Larson said. "Brad gave me a good push on the last restart for the lead, and from there I just had to hold them off. With three to go, I remember thinking that finally it's going to work out. It did. I was extremely excited."

Larson is far from the first driver to wrestle with the concept of scoring high finishes but missing the golden ring. While pursuing that

Larson's mother, Janet Miyata Larson, is Japanese American. Her parents were held in an internment camp during World War II because of government fears that Americans of Japanese heritage might hurt the Allied cause.

elusive first win, some have overdriven during the final laps, dusting the wall or slipping in turns while trying to manufacture results in a frantic environment that often isn't conducive to dramatic moves.

"There's no denying when you're young and new that it's easy to overdrive and make mistakes and cost yourself wins," Larson said. "It's easy to chase something that's out in front of you and make a mistake. It just depends on how close you are to the lead. It's circumstantial."

The Michigan victory, so long in coming, demanded some kind of celebration beyond the typical victory lane. Will Gray, engine tuner for the Chip Ganassi team, stepped in.

"He was like the party guy," Larson said with a certain amount of amusement. "We flew home from Michigan, and everybody went to his house. I think our IT guy sent out a mass email to everybody at Chip Ganassi Racing, including by accident the Indy Car team.

In 2020, Larson accomplished a major career goal by winning the Chili Bowl, one of short-track racing's marquee events, after more than a decade of attempts. He called it the biggest win of his life.

"Fifty or sixty people showed up. It was cool to get everybody from our race team there. A lot of people from the shop came by just to celebrate a little because you're never going to have a first Cup win again."

And the trophy, the one that was so hard to get? Larson was building a house that season and was dealing with the chaos inherent to that process, so the Michigan prize wound up in a storage unit. It's still there.

The win didn't mean Larson would enjoy an immediate cascade of other victories. Four wins followed in 2017, and he seemed to have found solid footing among the sport's elite, but 2018 resulted in a winless season. He won once in 2019, finishing sixth in points.

Then came 2020 and a critical error that almost cost Larson his chance at continuing big-time success. Four races into the Cup season, while competing during a live iRacing broadcast, Larson uttered the N-word. Flames followed. Quicker than a lap at Bristol, his sponsors

Kyle Larson celebrates after winning at Michigan. *John Harrelson*

disappeared and he lost the Ganassi ride. NASCAR, very alert and sensitive to such transgressions, suspended him.

Larson returned to dirt-track racing, where he rang up win after win over a stretch of almost one hundred races and, not incidentally, found a place of refuge and healing. And he began rebuilding his reputation, undergoing NASCAR-mandated sensitivity training and working with a diversity coach and Black athletes who shared their perspectives.

Along the way, Larson edged back into discussions with movers and shakers at the top levels of NASCAR, including team owner Rick Hendrick and retired driver and Hendrick lieutenant Jeff Gordon, the former short-track star who had paved the way for Larson and others to jump into NASCAR.

Convinced that Larson had learned a hard lesson and certain of his superstar potential, Hendrick hired him for the 2021 season. Larson responded almost immediately, winning in the schedule's fourth race (at Las Vegas) and scoring three consecutive victories in the middle part of the season on the way to his first Cup championship.

CHAPTER 8

David Pearson

Charlotte (NC) Motor Speedway, May 28, 1961

Years after he retired from driving race cars, David Pearson remained amazed at the daily contents of his mailbox.

The letters came from across the country—and across the oceans. Many were addressed simply to "David Pearson, Race Car Driver, Spartanburg, SC." Most held requests for autographs. Some writers simply wanted Pearson to know they were fans and that they hoped he enjoyed his retirement.

Pearson won three NASCAR Cup championships and 105 races in a career that began in 1960 and ended in 1986 (he tried to return in 1989 but "officially" retired after a practice session because of back problems). He is enshrined in numerous racing Halls of Fame, twice was named the American Driver of the Year, and was named Driver of the Century (the twentieth) by *Sports Illustrated*.

Pearson's crypt (he died in 2018) in Greenlawn Memorial Gardens in his hometown of Spartanburg makes no mention of his heroics on track but carries this short, meaningful message: Simply the Best.

Pearson didn't win as many races as Richard Petty or as many championships as Petty, Dale Earnhardt, and Jimmie Johnson, and he wasn't as in-your-face as Darrell Waltrip or Kyle Busch, but many who saw all the top drivers over the years will decorate Pearson as, indeed, the best.

He began proving himself in May 1961 at Charlotte Motor Speedway. Pearson had raced in his own cars in 1960, his debut season in Cup racing, and had turned enough heads to win the season's Rookie of the Year Award. But there were no wins and not much money, and Pearson looked to 1961 as a possible make-or-break season. For that to happen, he needed a real chance in a top-flight car, and the opportunity arrived in May. He was roofing a house in Spartanburg when Ray Fox, one of the sport's top crew chiefs, called offering Pearson a ride in the May 28 World 600 at Charlotte. Pearson was aware of Fox's excellent reputation and jumped at the chance to drive a solid race car.

After a practice session at Charlotte, Pearson drove onto pit road. Fox came over to the car and asked Pearson how it was running. "I don't know," he said. "I've never driven a race car that fast."

Pearson wasn't intimidated. "I was sitting in the car getting ready to start the race," he remembered in an interview years later. "Guys like Fireball Roberts and Joe Weatherly were up at the front. I said to myself, 'This car doesn't know who's driving it. If they can do it, I can do it.'"

And he did. Pearson pushed the Pontiac to the front and led 225 of the race's four hundred laps, including the final 129. He had a four-lap lead on Roberts with two laps to go in NASCAR's longest race when his right rear tire blew. Pearson stayed on the track and crossed the finish line with sparks flying from the car's right rear rim. Roberts finished second two laps down.

Wood Brothers team member Eddie Wood taped pieces of chewing gum on the dashboard of Pearson's cars. Pearson picked up a new piece every hundred miles. "It helped because your mouth would get so dry," Pearson said. "And it was always Wrigley's Spearmint."

Pearson had his first of 105 Cup victories and was on his way to decades of glory days at the top level of American auto racing. The Fox

David Pearson broke into victory lane in 1961 and retired with 105 victories. *David Griffin*

team won $24,280 that day at Charlotte, and Pearson used his share to buy a house in Spartanburg. Never in Pearson's wildest dreams had he thought of paying cash for a house. "I was just a mill-town boy, but, man, I was uptown after that win," Pearson said. Money wouldn't be an issue for him for the rest of his days.

"It was the biggest race I've ever won, and I reckon it always will be because it was the first big race I won," Pearson said years later. "I kept thinking during the race that I was in a dream or something because I was outrunning Fireball and all the other people. It was the best feeling in the world when I finally crossed the finish line and they waved the checkered flag. I guess I was as happy right then as I've ever been in my life."

Pearson would drive on to become the second-winningest driver (behind Petty's 200) in Cup history. He won the series championship in 1966, 1968, and 1969 but had his most spectacular seasons in the 1970s driving for the Wood Brothers team. In 1973, the year he picked as his best, he won eleven of eighteen starts in the Woods' cars with the famous No. 21 gold-foil number.

Pearson's biggest win came in the 1976 Daytona 500. He and Petty, his biggest rival throughout his career, crashed in Turn Four racing for the win with the checkered flag in sight. Both cars spun out. Pearson alertly used his clutch to keep his engine fired, and he recovered from the spin to limp across the finish line at about 30 miles per hour.

The 500 win was a vivid example of Pearson's keen intelligence on racetracks. He studied other drivers' strengths during races and often protected his equipment and tires to be stronger than everyone else at the end of a race. He earned the nickname Silver Fox both because of his on-track cunning and his salt-and-pepper hair.

"You figure out how fast everybody else is running," he said. "You see if you can beat them through the corners. I'd drop back and run with one and then the other. You're figuring them out and seeing where you can beat them."

Legendary driver, crew chief, and mechanic Cotton Owens, like Pearson

Pearson was never injured in a race car. His worst wreck occurred at Bristol Motor Speedway when contact with another car sent him into the wall. "I didn't get hurt, but it scared me because it knocked my shoes off," Pearson said. "I had always heard that when people were killed in a car wreck it knocked their shoes off. I didn't know if I was dead or not."

a member of the NASCAR Hall of Fame, once said Pearson could drive "anything, anywhere, anytime. He got in an Indy car during a tire test in Atlanta in the 1960s and was running a second faster than the other guys on his third lap. Then he got out and said he didn't like it. He could get out of one car and get in another and drive it faster than the guy who had been in it."

CHAPTER 9

Fireball Roberts

Occoneechee (NC) Speedway, Aug. 13, 1950

Edward Glenn "Fireball" Roberts Jr. had perhaps the all-time best auto racing nickname.

Oddly, it was a product of another sport.

Roberts picked up the Fireball moniker as a teenager when a baseball teammate caught one of his pitches and excitedly proclaimed it a "fireball." The name stuck.

Soon, it would be stitched onto racing uniforms worn by one of the fastest men alive.

In a hard sort of irony, the name rode with Roberts into the May 1964 race crash that ultimately ended his life. He was burned across most of his body in a fiery accident during the World 600 at Charlotte Motor Speedway and died of an infection about six weeks later.

In a short (1950–1964) racing career, Roberts, in the view of many, became NASCAR's first superstar driver. He was smart, steady, and very, very fast, and he was fearless and dominant on stock car racing's growing collection of super-fast asphalt superspeedways. No less a source than revered mechanic and racing innovator Smokey Yunick called Roberts "the best driver I ever had."

Journalist Max Muhleman, who covered much of Roberts's career and became a close friend, called the driver "one of the first guys—maybe the first—to become a big winner by using brains and discipline as well as bravery and extra skill levels. When asphalt tracks arrived, Fireball recognized the technique was different and adapted to it in a very thoughtful and calculated way, as well as using the skills that take you far in dirt track racing."

Roberts attended the University of Florida for two years with intentions of becoming a mechanical engineer, but racing showed him another path.

Roberts's star saw its first rise on an August day in 1950 at the now-defunct Occoneechee Speedway in Hillsborough, North Carolina. A fast and frightening dirt track of almost one mile in length, Occoneechee was one of the most challenging layouts of the day, and Roberts won there in only his third Cup race, outrunning dirt-track legend Curtis Turner, who finished second.

Roberts didn't win again in Cup (he concentrated on Modified racing through most of the 1950s) until 1956, when he scored five victories. In 1958, he won the Northern 500 at Trenton, New Jersey, and the Southern 500 in Darlington, South Carolina, to become the first driver to win two five-hundred-mile races in one season.

The Florida Sportswriters Association named Roberts its Professional Athlete of the Year, a signal honor for a racer.

When the huge Daytona International Speedway opened in 1959, it seemed built with Roberts in mind. He took to its high banks and never-before-seen speeds as if he had been born to race there, winning seven races, including the 1962 Daytona 500, over a five-year span at the track.

By 1964, Roberts's speed—he also was a master at big-track qualifying, which then rewarded drivers who drove all the way to the ragged edge—and style had made him a breakthrough star. He was featured in *Sports Illustrated* magazine, a rare thing for a stock car racer in those days, and became a symbol of the sport, particularly for marginal sports fans who knew little about auto racing. A guy with a very visible nickname and victories now running into the dozens logically attracted attention.

Roberts's ex-wife Doris (they married in 1950 after dating for three weeks but divorced fourteen years later) grew up attending races and was naturally attracted to race car drivers but said Glenn—she always called him Glenn—was a different sort of daredevil.

"What really attracted me to Glenn was his intelligence," she said in an interview in 2000, four years before her death. "I liked the things he liked. His manner. He was so intelligent. I had known a lot of race drivers through my brother, but I kept thinking, 'Hey, this man is a race driver.' He could talk about everything. He liked classical music, and so did I.

"He told me, 'I will be a champion.' I believed him. He had what it took to do what he wanted to do. He far surpassed the goals he set for himself."

Roberts, who was engaged to another woman in 1964, planned to retire from driving after running a few of the NASCAR tour's bigger races that season. He had reached an agreement to be a spokesman for a national brewing company and was working on putting that plan into motion when he arrived at Charlotte Motor Speedway for that year's World 600.

Only eight laps into the race, Roberts was swept into the accident that ultimately took his life. Ned Jarrett and Junior Johnson crashed in front of him, and Roberts slid to the inside before hitting the wall. His car flipped onto its roof, and the fuel tank exploded. Gasoline spilled into the car's cockpit and ignited.

Jarrett climbed from his car and raced toward Roberts, who was on fire and pleading for help. Jarrett

Roberts, who was inducted into the NASCAR Hall of Fame in 2014, didn't run enough races to seriously contend for the Cup championship in any season. Along with Junior Johnson, Mark Martin, and Dale Earnhardt Jr., he is remembered as one of the best drivers to never win a seasonal title.

pulled him from the car and started tearing off his uniform. Safety workers soon arrived, and Roberts was on the way to a Charlotte hospital, where he would be treated over the next month. He rallied several times but fell victim to pneumonia and a bloodstream infection. He died July 2, 1964, as the NASCAR tour was gathering at Daytona Beach for the track's annual summer race.

Roberts, who grew up in Daytona Beach, was laid to rest at the town's Bellevue Memorial Gardens, where visitors to his crypt, on race days, can hear the sound of race car engines at the nearby speedway. According to a plaque at his crypt, "he brought to stock car racing a freshness, distinction, a championship quality that surpassed the rewards collected by the checkered flag."

After Roberts's death, race innovators developed a fuel cell to guard against fires in race cars.

CHAPTER 10

Cale Yarborough

Valdosta (GA) 75 Speedway, June 27, 1965

I n the world of race car drivers, there is tough, and then there is Cale Yarborough tough.

Cale Yarborough tough is another level, right up there with A. J. Foyt tough.

Let Pete Hamilton, once a key challenger to Yarborough when Cale drove Wood Brothers Mercurys and Hamilton was in Petty Enterprises Plymouths, offer a description.

"Probably the guy I battled with more than anybody else was Cale Yarborough," Hamilton said in an interview years after their glory days. "We had some pretty tough fights in a lot of different places. One that comes to mind was at Michigan.

"We banged fenders all day long. At the end, he got paid for first. It was his determination. In those days we didn't have side glasses or window netting, so you could look over at the other guy going down the straightaway. I remember looking over at Cale. Even at 185 miles per hour, you could see the determination in his eyes."

That race was at Michigan International Speedway on June 7, 1970. Yarborough took the lead from Hamilton with two laps to go and out-ran him by 0.3 of a second at the finish.

Cale Yarborough scored his first win in 1965 and drove on to win three series championships in the 1970s. *BILL NIVEN / BRH RACING ARCHIVES*

It was one of eighty-three Cup victories Yarborough would score across a driving career that stretched from 1957 to 1988. He was the first driver to win three consecutive Cup championships (1976–1978). He won the Daytona 500 four times and the Southern 500 five times. Among many notable Yarborough statistics: he led 21 percent of the laps he raced.

Yarborough's first win came under unusual circumstances. He was scheduled to drive a Ford owned by Kenny Myler in a two-hundred-lap Cup race at Valdosta, Georgia, June 26, 1965. But bad weather trapped Yarborough in Charlotte, North Carolina, and he couldn't make the trip to southern Georgia. Sam McQuagg started the race in Myler's car, but rain halted the event after twenty-five laps, causing a postponement to the next day.

Standard NASCAR procedures call for races that are interrupted by rain to resume on the next clear day at the point at which they were halted. For whatever reason, the Valdosta race restarted at lap one the next day, and Yarborough, after driving from Charlotte and sleeping in his car (along with his wife and two daughters), was there. He led the

Two of Yarborough's Cup championship trophies were destroyed in a fire at his Florence, South Carolina, car dealership in 1988. He lost other racing memorabilia in 2007 when a propane tank explosion destroyed a workshop near his home.

last eighteen laps to break into the Cup winner's circle in his seventy-eighth career race.

If the race had resumed on the twenty-sixth lap, McQuagg would have been credited with the win because NASCAR considers the driver starting races as the "official" driver for the record.

The circumstances notwithstanding, Yarborough had established himself as a winner. Three years later, he scored what he has always considered his biggest win in the 1968 Southern 500 at Darlington Raceway, his "home" track and his favorite. That Labor Day afternoon was brutally hot, and photos of Yarborough in victory lane show his grimy face grinning through the exhaustion.

He was fully launched into a career that would make him an all-time stock car racing great.

Yarborough grew up on a farm in rural South Carolina and carried the work ethic he had learned as a youth into racing. He drove every lap as if his next meal depended on it. Sometimes, it did. He and his wife, Betty Jo, struggled through the early years on a wing and a prayer.

That brand of toughness was a throughline in Yarborough's career.

"He would not quit," said Junior Johnson, Yarborough's car owner during his championship seasons. "I think if he was in a situation where he had to get out of a race car because of his stamina, it would be the most embarrassing thing that ever happened to him.

"He was the most determined. There was no end to his willpower. He stood apart. He was smart. He was kind of 'sneaky' brave."

It is a reality of the television age that Yarborough's place in racing lore will be pegged not to his long list of accomplishments but to a race he didn't win—the 1979 Daytona 500. In one of the most famous NASCAR finishes of all time, Yarborough and Donnie Allison crashed while racing for the lead in the third turn on the final lap, opening

Cale Yarborough defined toughness as a three-time Cup champion.
Dick Conway

the door for Richard Petty to inherit the win. Yarborough and Allison, joined by Donnie's brother, Bobby, engaged in brief fisticuffs near their crashed cars, giving television viewers, many new to NASCAR, a quick tutorial in the sport's sometimes wild ways.

Remembering that day years later, Yarborough said, "I think it opened the world's eyes to stock car racing. I mean, they said, 'These

> Yarborough lived the definition of a mixed experience in qualifying for the 1983 Daytona 500. On the first of two laps, he ran the fastest qualifying lap in NASCAR history—200.503 mph. On the second lap, Yarborough's Chevrolet lost traction in the third turn, slid to the right, lifted into the air, and landed on its roof before slamming into the outside wall. He was frustrated but not injured.

guys are for real. They'll get out and duke it out if they have to.' The only regret I have is that it wasn't a better fight."

Yarborough and the Allisons settled their differences quickly and raced on.

A star athlete in high school, Yarborough could have followed any number of paths into adulthood. He seriously considered attending Clemson University on a football scholarship but eventually told Coach Frank Howard he wanted to pursue a career as a race car driver. "You'll starve to death, son," Howard told him.

Yarborough was pleased to prove Howard wrong, and they became fast friends, Howard later joining Yarborough in a victory lane celebration at Talladega Superspeedway, pulling him aside to admit that, yes, questioning the kid's career choice was a bad move.

Across the years, many competitors perhaps wished Yarborough had pursued that other game.

CHAPTER 11

Jimmie Johnson

Auto Club (CA) Speedway, Apr. 28, 2002

Almost every successful racer recalls a special moment that helped kick-start his or her career. A chance meeting with an owner looking for a driver. Maybe winning a short feature race on a weekly track that caught the eye of a series official. Or perhaps an open audition among a handful of promising young prospects.

For seven-time NASCAR Cup Series champion Jimmie Johnson, that "special" moment was the twenty hours he was at the bottom of a ravine after crashing his Chevrolet truck during the 1995 SCORE Baja International 1,000 off-road race along the Mexican peninsula.

Before Johnson's titles, his thirty-six poles, his eighty-three victories, and his almost inevitable selection to the NASCAR Hall of Fame, there was the Baja crash. It might seem a stretch, but Johnson credits that crash with helping him become the stock car driver he became.

It goes something like this:

In 1995, Johnson was nineteen and already making waves in stadium off-road and SCORE racing. Cocky to a fault, he had an attitude that even he later admitted was probably too much. That approach got him in trouble during the Tijuana-to-La Paz run down Mexico's treacherous Baja Peninsula.

Jimmie Johnson and his crew celebrate his seventh Cup championship at Homestead-Miami Speedway in 2016. *DAVID GRIFFIN*

It was nearing dawn, and Johnson was hoping daylight would keep him awake. Instead, he dozed off and crashed his No. 82 Chevrolet truck in the mountains, flipping and tumbling to the bottom of a deep ravine. "I kept wondering how far we were going to fall and how hard we were going to land," Johnson said several years ago. "I knew the possibility was there for a really bad situation. It's a moment I hope to never go through again."

Search teams needed twenty hours to find Johnson and his navigator, Tom Gieves, shaken but intact. Those hours might have been among the most important of Johnson's career. "During the time in that ravine I did a lot of soul-searching about how I raced," he said. "I learned a lot about myself out there. I was young and dumb and didn't really care if I crashed. I made a lot of mistakes and crashed a bunch because I wasn't afraid to stay on the gas all the time. I thought I needed that flash to get recognized.

"Maybe I fell into that [mindset] a little too much. I was crashing so much that my career was going in a bad direction. I was kind of known

Jimmie Johnson leads the field on the way to his first Cup victory in 2002 in Fontana, California. NIGEL KINRADE

as a reckless driver, viewed as someone no owner would want in his equipment because the crew would have to always fix it."

The Baja crash and subsequent off-season gave Johnson time to change his ways. He spent three more years in the dirt—and never got upside-down again. "In off-road terms, that's a pretty big statement . . . three years without getting upside-down," Johnson said. "That time out on the Baja thinking about what could have happened changed a lot in the way I went back racing."

Once he reined himself in, Johnson quickly went up America's motorsports ladder. He left off-road in 1998 to go stock car racing with the American Speed Association (ASA). Three years later he was in NASCAR's second-tier Xfinity Series with Chevrolet-based

Team Penske driver Ryan Newman edged Johnson for 2002 Cup Rookie of the Year. Newman had more poles and more top fives and top tens; Johnson had more victories and finished one points position better.

Herzog Motorsports. After watching Johnson in ASA and Xfinity cars, Cup Series champion Jeff Gordon convinced owner Rick Hendrick to hire Johnson. In 2002, Hendrick brought Johnson into Hendrick Motorsports, where he teamed with Gordon, Terry Labonte, Joe Nemechek, and Jerry Nadeau.

Gordon's assessment of the fellow Californian was spot-on. Johnson and crew chief Chad Knaus won in their thirteenth start, a 250-lap, five-hundred-miler in April of 2002 at California Speedway, near Johnson's hometown of El Cajon. They won eighty-two more races between 2002 and 2017, including a sixteen-year winning streak and a ten-victory season in 2007. Their unprecedented five consecutive championships came in 2006–2010. They scored again in 2013 and 2016.

Their first victory at Fontana came via late-race strategy. Johnson had qualified fourth and led three times for 48 of the first 235 laps. He got the lead again when Knaus called for gas-only during their last pit stop at lap 236. The quicker stop gave Johnson track position, an advantage he maintained the rest of the way to beat Kurt Busch.

Afterward, just as he did almost always, Johnson said all the right things. "Heck yeah," he said when asked whether he was surprised to win so quickly. "This is unbelievable. You always think you have the ability to be competitive, but you don't know until the right situation presents itself and you can showcase your talents. My hat's off to Chad Knaus. We're in a similar situation of trying to prove ourselves, and he's doing an awesome job. That was a great call to take no tires and gain track position."

Many fans' first memory of Johnson might have been his head-on crash and subsequent "Rocky" pose in the 2000 Xfinity race at Watkins Glen International.

The victory took some pressure off the Johnson/Knaus No. 48 Chevrolet team. "That's when I knew I was going to be employed," Johnson quipped afterward. "They said they'd be patient, that I had time [to develop], but in my heart I didn't think that was the case. I knew I needed to win, so to leave there with a trophy means I'd have a job for a few years."

"A few years" turned into twenty, but Johnson's slow goodbye from NASCAR was painful to watch. The last of his eighty-three victories came at Dover in June of 2017, one of three victories that year. He ended his career on a zero for one hundred thirty skid from mid-2017 through 2020. He had Knaus, Kevin Meendering, and Cliff Daniels atop his pit box at various times, but nothing seemed to click. (Daniels later became crew chief for 2021 Cup Series champion Kyle Larson.)

Johnson left NASCAR after 2020 to race Hondas for Chip Ganassi in the NTT IndyCar Series. He struggled in his twelve street and road races, never finishing better than seventeenth. He moved on to a full IndyCar schedule in 2022.

All of this (perhaps) because of those twenty soul-searching hours on the Baja Peninsula in 1995.

CHAPTER 12

Alan Kulwicki

Phoenix (AZ) International Raceway, Nov. 6, 1988

In his dual role as a race car driver and a race team owner, Alan Kulwicki was a man of details. Nothing was too small to get his attention.

It is no surprise, then, that Kulwicki put a lot of thought into what might happen when he won a Cup Series race for the first time, an accomplishment he and others were virtually certain would take place after he posted three top-five finishes in 1987, his first full season at the Cup level.

During the 1986 season, when Kulwicki was testing the waters in NASCAR after success on Midwestern short tracks, he had a conversation with long-time racing executive Humpy Wheeler, whose learned advice had been sought by numerous drivers over the years. Wheeler told Kulwicki that he should think about "separating" himself from other new drivers by creating a persona that would help him stand out from the others. Be different, he said.

Jump forward to the spring of 1988, with Kulwicki seemingly on the verge of a breakthrough moment. He clearly had taken Wheeler's advice to heart. During a talk with Tom Roberts, his public relations representative and race-day spotter, Kulwicki mentioned an idea he had been plotting.

Alan Kulwicki invented
the reverse victory
lap after scoring
his first win.
BARB SAUNDERS /
BRH RACING ARCHIVES

"He referred to it as a backward victory lap, or what he called a Polish victory lap," Roberts remembered. "I wasn't getting exactly what he was talking about. I was thinking he meant putting the car in reserve and going in reverse around the track. Was that a backward victory lap?

"I figured it out, and I thought it would be absolutely spectacular."

As drivers moved through the 1988 season, Kulwicki's self-made team stepped to the edge of absolute success—its first win. Kulwicki was fourth at Rockingham, second at super-tough Darlington, third at Charlotte, fifth at Bristol and Richmond, and second in the Martinsville five-hundred-lap marathon.

Then came Phoenix—the next-to-last race of the season. Everything clicked. Kulwicki led forty-one laps, including the final sixteen, and outran second-place Terry Labonte by a stunning margin—eighteen and one-half seconds—to finally enter victory lane.

Team owner and star driver, Alan Kulwicki famously did things "his way."
DICK CONWAY

"I was spotting for Alan up on Rattlesnake Hill [between Turns Three and Four]," Roberts said. "When he crossed the finish line and got on the back straight, I told him, 'Do your lap! Do your lap!' He slowed down as he was coming out of four, turned the car around and did his rendition of a victory lap. ESPN had gone to a commercial break, and when they came back, they showed him on the backward victory lap.

"I sprinted down to victory lane. I'm laughing, crying, screaming. After the Martinsville race, we knew it was just a matter of time. There had been so many close calls."

Alan Kulwicki's racing success is celebrated by the Alan Kulwicki Driver Development Program, which was started by a group of his friends in 2015. Directed by Tom Roberts, Kulwicki's public relations representative, the program chooses seven promising short-track drivers each year and supports their efforts monetarily and otherwise.

Kulwicki later said the backward lap had been high on his planning list for when the win finally came.

"It's something I had thought about a long time," he said. "I wanted to do something special. There would never be another first win. I wanted to give them something to remember me by."

The win, and everything else Kulwicki accomplished in a career that was all too brief, was scored with a skeletal crew. Only four team members made the trip west from his Charlotte shop; the rest of the crew was made up of Southwest and West Coast locals.

Kulwicki was an outlier in the NASCAR garage. One of the few drivers in NASCAR history with a college education, he held a mechanical engineering degree from the University of Wisconsin-Milwaukee. He called his education "essential in the success of operating my own team."

Kulwicki had beaten the best—teams with much bigger budgets and many more employees—with smarts, shortcuts, and no small amount of determination.

Alan Kulwicki started at the bottom of the ladder but eventually notched a Cup championship. Dick Conway

A background in engineering helped propel Alan Kulwicki to NASCAR success.
Dick Conway

After most races, Kulwicki was all about getting home and getting ready for the next one. On this Phoenix Sunday, however, it was time to celebrate.

"We wound up having the damnedest party that night at the Embassy Suites at the [Phoenix] airport," Roberts said. "Somewhere there must be pictures. People who were there still talk about it as one helluva celebration party. It was 3:00 a.m. before I left, and people were still partying."

Kulwicki had proven that he could do things his way and be successful. He had been offered rides with prominent teams (including the juggernaut run by Junior Johnson) but was determined to put his own team among the elite. And he did it without the cash and flash of the sport's giants.

"I believe in providing for necessities rather than worry about luxuries," he once said. "I don't agree that having the most employees, the biggest and most elaborate race shop and the most race cars are the most important factors in this sport. None of that spells success on the race-track. You can only race one car and engine at a time. And it isn't the sheer numbers of people employed in a business that makes it successful. It's the number who are actually working and achieving that counts."

Kulwicki carried that philosophy to the Cup championship in 1992. He rallied in the final event of the season, winning the title by ten points over Bill Elliott in one of the most memorable races in the sport's history.

Sadly, Kulwicki's championship celebration was cut short. On April 1 of the next season, he and four associates were killed in the crash of their private plane as it attempted to land near Bristol, Tennessee, for that weekend's race.

The Bristol track was cloaked in mourning the next day. Kulwicki's team withdrew from the race. Peter Jellen, the team's truck driver, drove the team transporter around the track, tears in his eyes, and NASCAR flagman Doyle Ford waved the checkered flag as he crossed the finish line.

CHAPTER 13

Davey Allison

Talladega (AL) Superspeedway, May 3, 1987

It seemed only appropriate that Davey Allison, an Alabamian through and through, scored his first NASCAR Cup Series victory in May 1987 at Talladega Superspeedway, the giant track located fifty miles east of Birmingham.

It's a horrible irony that Allison, son of one of the sport's superstars and a champion in the making, lost his life at the same track six years later.

Between those days, Davey fulfilled many of the considerable expectations that shadowed him from the day he first climbed into a race car. Older son of Bobby Allison, a Hall of Famer and often considered one of the five best drivers in the history of the sport, Davey arrived in stock car racing with a hard-earned degree from the University of Bobby. He climbed in and on and under his father's race cars virtually from the time he was able to walk, and there was little doubt, within the family and inside the sport, that he would follow Bobby along the same avenue that seemed to attract every Allison who sat behind a windshield.

At twenty-six, only fourteen races into his Cup career and still in his rookie season, Davey won the Winston 500 at Talladega, becoming the first rookie to claim a Cup victory in six years. And, in a circumstance

Son of a great champion, Davey Allison scored his first Cup victory at Talladega Superspeedway. *JERRY HAISLIP / BRH ARCHIVES*

that had the word "fate" written all over it, his father's car crashed into the frontstretch fence during that race, spraying parts and pieces into the grandstand and halting the race for almost three hours. Bobby was not seriously injured, but Davey didn't know that as he watched the wild wreck unfold in his rear-view mirror.

"When I looked up in the mirror and saw Dad going into the fence, it was the emotional low period of my life," Davey said after the race.

Although shaken, Bobby watched the rest of the race from the top of a motor home in the infield, witness to his son's first victory.

It was a wild weekend at Talladega. In qualifying, Bill Elliott set a stock car speed record of 212.809 miles per hour in winning the pole. After Allison's car took flight during the race and came within a few strong fence sections of sailing into the grandstand, ever-increasing speeds resulted in NASCAR putting restrictor plates on engines for future events at the tour's fastest tracks.

Davey led much of the race but saw the finish come down to a ten-lap shootout. NASCAR shortened the race from 188 laps to 178 because the long delay to repair the frontstretch fence pushed the event into near darkness. Allison left the pits after the final caution one spot behind leader Dale Earnhardt Sr., but he passed Earnhardt, a master at Talladega, quickly and led the rest of the way.

Allison also would win at Dover, Delaware, that season on the way to claiming the Cup Rookie of the Year award.

The next season put father and son together in the headlines again as Bobby finished first and Davey second in an all-Allisons Daytona 500. Years later, Davey would recall the race as one of the special moments of his career.

In an interview in the summer of 1991, Davey said he patterned his career and his life after his father.

"People react differently to things because their personality dictates it, but I think I had a good example to follow the way he handles himself around people and the media, on the race track and away from the race track," he said. "He has been a big influence on my life, not just the racing part of it but the personal, as well."

Davey was inducted into the NASCAR Hall of Fame in 2019, joining his father as one of only seven father-son duos in the hall.

Larry McReynolds, who served as Allison's crew chief during much of his success, said Davey and Bobby were very similar in their determination. "They're both a little hard-headed," McReynolds said. "That maybe got Bobby in more hot water than it did Davey, but Bobby had a longer period of time to get in hot water. But their hard-headedness normally paid dividends."

Allison, driving for Robert Yates Racing, finished third in the Cup point standings in 1991 and started 1992 in grand style, winning the Daytona 500. He won the All-Star Race at Charlotte in a spectacular finish, crossing the finish line first as his car collided with that of Kyle

While in high school, Allison bagged groceries from 3:30 to 9:00 p.m. before heading to work on the night shift at his father's race shop.

A victory threat on tracks both small and large, Davey Allison inherited his father's expertise in building race cars. DICK CONWAY

Petty. Allison spent the night in a nearby hospital with a bruised lung and a concussion, missing the post-race celebration.

That season was a mix of success and trouble for Allison, who seemingly either won or suffered an injury. The worst day came at Pocono Raceway in Pennsylvania, where contact with Darrell Waltrip sent Allison's Ford into a series of flips and spins. He suffered a broken arm, wrist, and collarbone.

The injured Allison raced on with the help of relief drivers and took the series point lead into the final race at Atlanta. He lost a shot at the championship—which was won by Alan Kulwicki—when his car was seriously damaged in a crash with Ernie Irvan.

Most people in racing assumed Allison, who had totaled nineteen Cup wins, would have many other chances to win a championship, but those dreams came to a tragic end in July 1993 when a helicopter he was piloting crashed while landing in the infield at Talladega Superspeedway. Allison, thirty-two, died of severe head injuries the next day.

Virtually the entire state of Alabama fell into public mourning, the kind of traumatic reaction not seen there since the death of beloved

As a twenty-year-old, Allison raced on the short-track All Pro circuit with help from a group of young volunteers who became known as the Peachfuzz Gang.

University of Alabama football coach Bear Bryant in 1983. Race team owner Robert Yates skipped the next race, saying Allison's crew could not race "with tears in our eyes."

McReynolds, one of Allison's closest friends, said the driver "was still climbing. We don't have a crystal ball or live in a what-if world, but I feel very strongly he would have won a lot more races and there probably are drivers who wouldn't have the number of championships they have now."

CHAPTER 14

Kurt Busch

Bristol (TN) Motor Speedway, Mar. 24, 2002

The half-mile monstrosity that is Bristol Motor Speedway (BMS) has a well-earned reputation as one of NASCAR's "heartbreaker" tracks. No matter how good the driver, how smart the crew chief, how reliable the equipment, or how solid the strategy, the high-banked concrete track in eastern Tennessee will still beat you up in a split-second. The old saying "You can run, but you can't hide" applies perfectly to BMS.

Still, former NASCAR Cup Series champion Kurt Busch loves the place. "Maybe not for others," said Busch, a six-time winner at the so-called Last Great Colosseum, "but Bristol and I have gotten along pretty well for many, many years. I always look forward to going there twice a year."

Of Bristol's thirty-eight Cup winners in 121 races dating to 1961, only five got their first career victory there. Dale Earnhardt was the first, in April of 1979. Rusty Wallace did it in April of 1986, Ernie Irvan in August of 1990, and Elliott Sadler in March of 2001. Busch was the most recent of the five, getting his initial career victory there in March of 2002. It was the sixth race of the season, the weekend before the annual spring Easter break.

Kurt Busch's breakthrough win at Bristol was his first of four victories in the 2002 season. *David Griffin*

Perhaps surprisingly, some of NASCAR's all-time best drivers have struggled at BMS. Seven-time champion and eighty-three-time winner Jimmie Johnson won only twice in thirty-eight Bristol starts. Former three-time champion Tony Stewart was one for thirty-three and former champions Dale Jarrett and Bill Elliott were both one for forty-four. Ricky Rudd was winless in fifty-eight starts, the three Bodine brothers were a combined zero for eighty-two, and the two Burton brothers were a combined one for sixty-five.

Clearly, Bristol Motor Speedway is not for everyone.

On the other hand: Darrell Waltrip once won seven straight five-hundred-lap races en route to twelve victories in his fifty-two career starts at Bristol. Earnhardt, Wallace, and Cale Yarborough each won there nine times. Both of the Busch brothers have done well: Kyle with eight victories and Kurt with six. The most recent winners were Joey Logano in the 2021 dirt race and reigning Cup Series champion Kyle Larson in the 2021 race that helped set the sixteen-driver playoff field.

Like most drivers, Kurt Busch needed a couple of shaky starts to get somewhat comfortable at Bristol. Driving the No. 97 Ford for

Roush Fenway Racing (RFR), he started thirty-ninth and finished a next-to-last forty-second in his Bristol debut in April of 2001. "I think I wrecked three times in that first race," he recalled. "We eventually ran out of radiators, so I couldn't go back out after the last wreck. To be honest, I was scared and intimidated that first time. But when my sponsor [Sharpie] picked up the night race, I figured I'd better figure out how to get around the track in a hurry."

He did so in relatively quick order: he started twenty-sixth and finished twenty-fifth in August of 2001, an uneventful ten laps behind. He then won the March of 2002 race over Jimmy Spencer and was sixth in that year's fall race. Clearly, the older of the racing brothers from Las Vegas was getting to know Bristol a bit better. For proof, consider his victories for Roush Fenway Racing in both five-hundred-lap races in March and August of 2003. (He also won for RFR in April of 2004, for Team Penske in March of 2006, and for Stewart-Haas Racing in August of 2018.)

Busch's career resume is clearly Hall of Fame–worthy: 2004 Cup Series champion, forty victories at seventeen different tracks, including a Daytona 500.

"It was really huge to win here for the first time in 2002," Busch said last year. "When fans ask about my wins, I tell them the 2002 spring Bristol race is my all-time favorite. [This from a man with a Daytona 500 trophy.] You never forget your first one, especially at a special place like this. To be honest about it, I was intimidated at first; it scared me when I first came in here. When you walk in for the first time and look at that banking and how tight the track is, you can't help but being a little intimidated."

Busch started twenty-seventh on the Sunday of his first career victory. He and crew chief Jimmy Fennig agree to gas-only during their last pit stop. "We were getting such good wear that we went for a quicker stop by not changing tires," Fennig said in victory lane. "That's what helped [Elliott] Sadler win last year for the Wood Brothers. We went 152 laps on the last set today. Kurt did an awesome job; he's the man."

The victory came in Busch's forty-eighth career start, only his third at Bristol. "But the car felt really good in practice that weekend," he said. "I thought, 'WOW! This is really good.' It was a unique feel, something I'd never felt before at Bristol. Jimmy had put in the same setup he and Mark Martin had always used here. I don't know if my driving style was that close to Mark's, but it worked. There was so much grip on corner exit. Jimmy said, 'That's how you roll the center of the corner to keep up your speed.'

One of Busch's best outings was his sixth-place finish in the 2014 Indy 500 for Andretti Autosport, good enough for Rookie of the Year.

"We had a little body damage [who doesn't at Bristol?], so I raced smart and worked my way back to the front. [He led twice for 89 of the 500 laps, including the final 56.] I ran down [leader] Jimmy Spencer and moved him out of the way [at lap 444], then ran like a rabbit the rest of the way. Jimmie Johnson once said that Dover felt slow to him. Well, Bristol feels slow to me. I don't know why . . . it's hard to explain, but that's the way it felt."

Busch was twenty-three and living large at the time. He recalled that breakthrough night with great fondness. "It was like reaching the top of Mount Everest," he said. "You look around and you're the only one up there . . . and it's taken all your life to get there. We were off the next weekend, so I went to Virginia Beach with some friends and partied all week."

CHAPTER 15

Ricky Rudd

Riverside (CA) Raceway, June 5, 1983

NASCAR would never allow such a thing these days, but racing was a bit more relaxed and unscripted the weekend Ricky Rudd made his first Cup Series start in early March of 1975. The Chesapeake, Virginia, native was just eighteen when long-time Cup Series owner/ driver Bill Champion took him to the North Carolina Motor Speedway at Rockingham for the Carolina 500.

Not only was it to be Rudd's inaugural Cup Series start, but it also was to be his first competitive start in *any kind* of racing vehicle.

Strange but true: Rudd had absolutely zero experience when he started the 492-lap, 500-mile endurance grind at the 1.017-mile track in the Sandhills of North Carolina. He'd never turned a single lap of competition in any type of four-wheel racing vehicle, yet there he was debuting. No clunker car on a weekend short track. Certainly nothing as "real" as a Late Model. He'd never attended a formal driving school or had any personal coaching by a stock car veteran. He'd never raced for a rival stock car series or done any racing on a simulator. Maybe a motocross or two, but that hardly prepared him for what was to come.

It's nothing short of amazing that NASCAR officials would approve Champion's request to let the fuzzy-cheeked kid on the grid

Ricky Rudd's racing career had an unusual start—his first race of any sort was in the Cup Series. *DICK CONWAY*

with superstars like Cale Yarborough, Richard Petty, David Pearson, and Buddy Baker.

Earlier that year Champion and Virginia businessman Al Rudd had taken Ricky and his older brother, Al Jr., across Hampton Roads Harbor to Langley Speedway in Hampton. There, on a Wednesday morning, Champion hoped one of the brothers would show enough potential to perhaps succeed him when he retired from his No. 10 Ford. Ricky was somewhat better than Al that day—they took turns during the one-car audition, leading Champion and Rudd Sr. to pick Ricky for the Rockingham race. Against all odds, the youngster would dive head-first into NASCAR against forty-one pros, few of whom even knew his name.

Rudd calls the 1997 Brickyard 400 victory his best NASCAR moment but also favors his 1992 IROC championship based on two second-place finishes and two thirds in the four-race series.

Looking even younger than his eighteen years, the recent high school graduate started twenty-sixth in the Carolina 500. He was lapped an astonishing fifty-six times before finishing eleventh and earning $2,000. As unlikely as it may have seemed that day, a Hall of Fame–worthy career was born.

Nine winless seasons and 160 starts later, in June of 1983, Rudd dominated the Budweiser 400 at Riverside Raceway in Southern California. His first career victory also was the first for Hall of Fame owner Richard Childress and crew chief Kirk Shelmerdine. Their No. 3 Piedmont Airlines Chevrolet started fourth, led four times for fifty-seven of the ninety-five laps—including the final forty-one laps—easily beating Bill Elliott on the road course. The margin of victory was seven seconds, the winner's payout $24,530.

In the fall of 1996, more than twenty-one years after finishing fifty-six laps behind in his NASCAR debut, Rudd won the AC Delco 400 at the North Carolina Motor Speedway near Rockingham.

"It was hard to believe I was finally able to win," said Rudd, now a youngish-looking sixty-six. "I'd been close a few times, with poles and good runs and strong finishes with other teams. But to have it all come together that afternoon . . . it was like an impossible feat finally happening. I didn't have any engine problems, the car was excellent, and pit stops were good. I couldn't have asked for anything more."

At the time, Rudd admitted that he'd been painfully unprepared for his Cup debut nine years earlier. "I had a steep learning curve in those big, heavy stock cars because I'd never done any short-track racing," he said. "It took me longer to figure out how to win, to figure out what was going on. Richard Childress helped by taking me to a [non-NASCAR] race in Texas the winter before the 1983 season. He wanted to instill in me what it took to win. There were some heavy-hitters there, but we won. That really helped my confidence."

The Riverside victory came in the sixth of his sixteen visits to the road course near Los Angeles. He won there for Bud Moore in 1985 and had seven other top-ten finishes at the track. All told, six of Rudd's twenty-three career victories came on road courses, spread evenly among Riverside, Sears Point, and Watkins Glen.

"I always looked forward to going out and racing on the West Coast," he said. "To me, that meant I had sort of reached the big time. Not that racing in the Southeast wasn't a big deal, but California was hot-rod country, and I enjoyed being out there. It seemed special to go across country to race."

It wasn't surprising that Rudd struggled early in his career. He spent the 1975–1980 seasons on teams with limited resources and mid-pack equipment. But he was impressive enough to earn a season with DiGard Racing, two winning seasons with RCR, four with Bud Moore Engineering, two with Kenny Bernstein's young team, and four with Hendrick Motorsports. He fielded his own Rudd Performance Motorsports from 1994 to 1999, getting his most memorable victory at the 1997 Brickyard 400.

He closed his thirty-three-year career with three seasons each with Robert Yates and the Wood Brothers and a final season (2007) back at Yates after sitting out 2006. His career record: 906 starts, twenty-nine poles, twenty-three victories, and sixteen consecutive winning seasons. Behind those numbers: 788 consecutive starts, which was second all-time to Jeff Gordon's 797. There were nineteen top-ten points seasons, including second to Earnhardt in 1991. He won at fourteen venues for six owners, including giving Childress and Bernstein their first Cup victories. And he was 1977 Rookie of the Year for his self-owned family team.

"Riverside was important, but Indy was my biggest win," Rudd said. (It's the only trophy displayed in his home; the others are stored in the attic.) "Winning Riverside and later that season at Martinsville sort of sealed things for the future. I had started to wonder if I was somebody who couldn't close the deal. You know, could qualify and run strong, but just couldn't win. It was a great day because after getting a taste of winning, the rest of them came easier."

CHAPTER 16

Rex White

Champion (NC) Speedway, Nov. 3, 1957

For former NASCAR Cup Series champion Rex White, it was love at first sight. Truly: Within the first few hours after watching racing for the first time, the North Carolina native decided to make NASCAR the center of his life.

Seventy-some years later, it still is.

It's likely that White is NASCAR's second-most *overlooked* champion, trailing only 1950 titlist the late Bill Rexford. But don't let White's casual, soft-spoken, gentlemanly demeanor fool you. A closer look reveals a highly successful, fiercely competitive, skillful driver who doesn't fit into any "superstar" category except one: he hated losing more than anything.

At ninety-three, he is NASCAR's oldest living champion, eight years past Richard Petty. Born in the hardscrabble year of 1929, White still lives on the same plot of rural land where he was reared in Taylorsville, North Carolina. He was in his early twenties, working in a gas station in Washington, DC, when he quite impulsively decided to become a racer.

"A man came in the station with posters advertising Lanham Speedway," White said. "I saved enough to go with my wife and her brother and his wife. I had no earthly idea what I was going to see. Lanham was the first time I'd ever seen a track and a car. It was in the early 1950s and stock car racing was just catching on."

It was a life-changing experience that led from pumping gas and checking oil to making the 2015 NASCAR Hall of Fame.

"The pits were outside, so you couldn't see the cars until they came out for practice," White recalled. "The first one was numbered 4-F. I don't know, maybe the driver hadn't passed his Army physical. He hadn't been out there long before I leaned over and told my brother-in-law, 'Right there; that's what I'm going to do.' I decided right then and there to become a racer."

Later that evening he slipped through the fencing and roamed the pits. He became a fan of Frankie Schneider, a local favorite and consistent winner. When Schneider's regular crewman went into the Korean War, White offered himself as a volunteer gofer. Once inside, racing became his passion.

This was shortly after Bill France moved to Daytona Beach, Florida, to begin promoting races along the beach south of town. Within a few years, White would become one of his biggest winners and earliest champions.

White's only superspeedway victory was a four-hundred-miler at Atlanta Motor Speedway in 1962.

And other than those inside NASCAR, hardly anyone noticed.

"It wasn't my nature to be the center of attention," White explained. "If a newspaper reporter came my way, I'd dodge him like a bulldog. I didn't realize how important publicity could be. But Fireball Roberts . . . if there was a sportswriter anywhere, he wouldn't have to look for Fireball. No, because Fireball would go find him. That wasn't my lifestyle. I just did my thing and didn't worry about being a star."

Frankly, White didn't exactly look the part. He's always been smallish in stature, maybe five foot five and 135 pounds on his best days. To many, he's almost a dead-ringer for TV personality and standup comedian the late George Goble. He was mild-mannered and agreeable when things were going well; aggressive and determined when they weren't. After surviving childhood polio, he walked and raced with a weakened right leg—not that it ever slowed him down.

Despite everything, he fulfilled his vow to become a championship racer. After success in non-NASCAR Sportsman races in the Northeast and Florida, he went Cup racing for owner Max Welborn in 1954. The first of his twenty-eight Cup victories came at Champion Speedway in Fayetteville, North Carolina, in November of 1957. It was a 150-lap, fifty-miler that officially opened the 1958 season.

"I remember a lot about that track, but not much about that first win," White said. "Fayetteville was a third-mile, high-banked, paved track that seemed to fit my style. I think somebody else [pole-starter Jack Smith] led most of the laps but fell out late [crashed]. I think [correctly] I led just the last five laps. I'd run some Sportsman races there, so I knew a few things about the track. That first win was a long, long time ago."

In the summer of 1966, two years after his final Cup start, White did a little short-track Sportsman racing. From Thursday night through Sunday afternoon, he won at Columbia, South Carolina; Asheville, North Carolina; North Wilkesboro, North Carolina; Shelby, North Carolina, and Spartanburg, South Carolina.

All but one of his victories came on short tracks and only three "winning tracks" remain on the schedule: Martinsville, Atlanta, and Richmond. "I'd like to have won more big-track races," White said, "because that's where the money was. A lot of guys today would like to win twenty-eight races. My banking account would be a whole lot better if I'd done that today. But it took horsepower to win on big tracks. It took the right shocks and springs and handling to win on short tracks. I think that's where I had it on some other drivers."

White won the 1960 Cup Series title in a most unusual manner. White and crew chief Louis Clements entered thirty-seven races with their own Chevrolet, and he got one-off rides from owners Beau Morgan, Scotty Cain, and L. D. Austin. Their forty combined entries scored 4,000-plus more points than Petty. White had more victories, top fives, and top tens, and won more money than anyone. He led the tour in laps completed, miles completed, lead-lap finishes, average start, and average finish. He had an astonishing thirty-five top tens in forty starts, including sixteen consecutive top tens to close the season.

His twenty-eight victories came during five seasons, between 1958 and 1962. Nobody else—neither of the Pettys, or Roberts, Ned Jarrett, Curtis Turner, Buck Baker, or Joe Weatherly—won as often during those years. In addition to his 1960 title, White was top ten in points six consecutive times during the height of his nine-year career. He won at least one pole in eight of those nine years.

"At the end, finances got to me," he said wistfully. "I had to quit racing and go back home and go to work to make some money. I had always done things pretty much my own way. Yeah, I made some mistakes, but I've had a pretty good life overall."

CHAPTER 17

A. J. Foyt

Daytona (FL) International Speedway, July 4, 1964

Think "A. J. Foyt" and the first thoughts that come to mind are four Indy 500 victories, victories in the long-distance sports car races at LeMans, Sebring, and Daytona Beach, a dozen USAC/CART national championship seasons, and sixty-seven USAC/CART Indycar victories.

Given those stats, it's understandable that his NASCAR Cup Series resume is often overlooked. It shouldn't be, for when Foyt was at the top of his game, he was as good as anybody has ever been in a stock car.

The legendary "Super Tex" had a NASCAR career that almost anybody racing today would love to have. He won nine Cup Series poles and seven superspeedway races in just 128 starts for a dozen team owners. Plus, he had twenty-two other top-five finishes and fourteen other finishes in the top ten. Six of his seven victories came in 400- or 500-mile races on long, fast ovals; the other was a grueling 505-miler on a demanding road course. There was nothing even remotely easy about any of them.

The first came more than fifty-eight years ago, in the July 1964 Firecracker 400 at Daytona International Speedway. Foyt, twenty-nine at the time, was in a cherry-red No. 47 Dodge owned by Ray Nichels

A. J. Foyt was known for success in open-wheel cars but also found victory lane in NASCAR. *Dick Conway*

and led by crew chief Crawford Clements. After starting nineteenth, he barely avoided a first-lap accident when seventeenth-starting Reb Wickersham spun across his nose nearing Turn One. Foyt recovered and went on to lead eight times for fourteen laps in just his tenth career NASCAR start.

Larry Foyt, A. J.'s son by adoption and grandson by birth, had a short and difficult NASCAR Cup Series career. He made twenty-three starts between 2000 and 2007 with only one top-twenty finish, a sixteenth at Homestead in 2003. Grandson A. J. Foyt IV gave up a promising open-wheel career when he married into the Irsay family of Indianapolis Colts fame. He's been part of the organization's scouting staff since 2010.

Astonishingly, he and teammate Bobby Isaac swapped the lead sixteen times in the final 55 of the 160 laps. Isaac had the better of it most of the time, leading 41 laps to Foyt's 14. But Foyt made a last-lap, three-wide, low-side pass to take the lead approaching Turn Three, then held on for the split-second victory.

"It's a heck of a feeling when you worry about two of your drivers getting each other in trouble," Nichels said after the 160-lap race. "But it sure makes you feel good to know they're running up front. That's the best racing duel I've ever seen. I had two of the very best out there in my cars."

Isaac and Foyt took the white flag together, with the lapped car of Paul Goldsmith (in relief of Jim Paschal) right with them. They went three-wide down the backstretch: Foyt inside, Isaac in the middle, Goldsmith outside. They stayed three-wide approaching Turn Three, where Foyt flirted with the apron to ease by and take the lead for good. He won the dash to the finish, arriving a half-length ahead of Isaac.

A. J. Foyt was an infrequent visitor to NASCAR events but usually brought strong cars when he entered races. *Dick Conway*

Foyt famously won the 24 Hours of LeMans in 1967, the only time he raced at the French track. Driving a Ford GT-40, he did an extra nighttime stint when co-driver Dan Gurney was unavailable for a scheduled driver change.

"I went way down, getting right to the apron, to pass Bobby going into Turn Three," Foyt recalled. "Art Lamey of Champion [Spark Plugs] told me later that he'd never seen numbers on top of a car until he saw my forty-seven in Turn Four."

Foyt told reporters at the time: "I didn't want to be ahead of Bobby starting the last lap [and risk having Isaac slingshot by entering Turn Three]. I managed to get by before we hit the corner, then held him off."

Foyt won the next year's four-hundred-miler for Wood Brothers Racing, beating Buddy Baker. He won the spring 1970 road race at Riverside, California, in a Ford from Jack Bowsher. His last four Cup victories came with the Wood brothers: 1971 at Ontario, California, and Atlanta, Georgia; 1972 at Daytona Beach (he won the 500 by more than a lap); and later in 1972 back at Ontario, California.

If not for licensing restrictions, Foyt would have run more NASCAR events. "The big ones I ran were all FIA-sanctioned," he explained. "I couldn't run the non-FIA races because I would have been barred from other series. I enjoyed the NASCAR races, but most of my time was with the open-wheel cars."

There was a stretch between 1964 and 1972 when Foyt was almost unbeatable in his occasional NASCAR starts: he had seven victories, twenty-one top-five finishes, and twenty-four top tens in only fifty starts. Throw in a dozen front-row starts and you have as impressive a stretch as any "NASCAR outsider" has ever enjoyed.

"We're pretty proud of our record with A. J.," said Wood Brothers Racing co-owner Eddie Wood. "We had him for twelve races during parts of 1965, then again in 1971 and 1972." (During those years Foyt also raced for Banjo Matthews, Jack Bowsher, Junior Johnson, and Holman-Moody). "He had seven poles, five wins, and was second, third, or fourth in five other races with us. Except for two DNFs, he never finished worse than fourth in one of our cars.

"And he didn't have a whole lot of NASCAR experience at our level. He'd run some USAC stock cars, but mostly he'd been in Indy cars and those light, quick little open-wheel cars. All of a sudden, he was in big, heavy full-bodied cars going real fast on big, paved, banked tracks with a lot of competition on all sides. When he came to us it worked out really, really well. Sort of like when [David] Pearson came to us after A. J. went back to IndyCar racing. We were fortunate enough to have two great, great drivers in our cars, one right after the other."

Foyt's NASCAR career began to wane after he and the Woods finished second to Baker at Texas World Speedway late in 1972. Between then and 1994 he made occasional starts with lagging results for his own team and several owners. His NASCAR involvement ended with a disappointing thirtieth in the inaugural Brickyard 400 in 1994. His final twenty years in stock cars were not especially noteworthy: zero poles, zero victories, nine top fives, and thirteen top tens in his last seventy-one starts.

But it speaks volumes about his skill set that he could occasionally jump into a stock car and show the NASCAR regulars exactly how it was done.

CHAPTER 18

Joey Logano

New Hampshire Motor Speedway, June 28, 2009

For years, former NASCAR Cup Series champion Joey Logano wouldn't let himself fully enjoy the memory of his first career victory. It came in June of 2009, when Logano was declared the winner of the rain-shortened Lennox Industrial Tools 301 at New Hampshire Motor Speedway in Loudon.

Nicknamed "Sliced Bread"—as in, "This Logano kid is the greatest thing since . . ."—the Connecticut teenager was just nineteen, easily the youngest driver on the forty-three-car grid. Loudon was just his twentieth Cup Series start, his eighteenth for Joe Gibbs Racing (JGR). Perhaps understandably, hardly anyone on the property that midsummer day expected much from him and crew chief Greg Zipadelli. Imagine their surprise when Logano and his team stole career victory No. 1 thanks to luck, good timing, and the weather.

"The fact it was rain-shortened took away some of the thrill," Logano said last year. "At the time, winning a rain race felt different from winning one that had gone full distance. But I look at it a little differently now, now that I've been around the sport twelve or thirteen years. I haven't had another rain-shortened victory, but I've had plenty that were lost to rain . . . so I'll take it because these things eventually even out."

Joey Logano rolled into Cup racing with great expectations and reached the circle of champions. *DAVID GRIFFIN*

There's no denying that Logano and Zipadelli got lucky. They had to overcome a wall-banging spin that cost them a lap at 184. A subsequent caution and its "lucky dog" wave-around put them back on the lead lap with plenty of racing remaining. Conservative fuel strategy helped build a three-to-five-second cushion as frontrunners pitted under green earlier than Logano and Zipadelli. All the while, weather-watchers were saying the race eventually would be impacted by rain.

After being mired deep in the field, Logano suddenly found himself ahead of the field when Ryan Newman pitted from the lead at lap 263. Moments later, just a handful of laps before Logano was scheduled for his final green-flag stop, the rain finally arrived. The race went under caution for a handful of laps before officials stopped it altogether with the red flag.

When it became clear the 301-lap race would end at 273, Logano suddenly found himself an unlikely Cup winner (over Jeff Gordon and Kurt Busch) for the first time. "Greg went for it and I was just lucky enough to be in the seat," Logano said afterward. "He said to stay out [because] rain was in the area. So, I started saving a little bit of fuel so I could go a little farther than everyone else. It's a dream come true, that's for sure."

On the other hand:

"But it's not the way you want to win your first race, in the rain, but twenty years down the road, when you look in the record books, no one will know the difference," Logano added. "Right now, I guess I'd rather be lucky than good. We didn't have the car to win, but we overcame a lot. A win is a win, and I'll take them any way I can."

Zipadelli, who had won thirty-three times with Tony Stewart, was as stunned as his rookie driver. "It's crazy," he said at the time. "Obviously, everything at the end of the day went our way. You can't control the weather; the only thing you can do is try to play it to your hand."

Two-time Xfinity Series champion and fellow Connecticut native Randy LaJoie is credited with giving Logano his "Sliced Bread" nickname.

Alas, Logano lost 104 more times before winning three years later at Pocono. He and Mark Martin swapped the lead five times in the final thirty-five laps before Logano won with a late pass. "That winning experience was everything you would hope for," he said. "It was so different from when I won the first one in the rain at Loudon. It was better in every way because it went the full four hundred miles. And it was very important at the time because I didn't know where I'd be racing the next year."

Logano's long-time nickname reflected his status as a teenaged, go-kart, quarter-midget, Legend, Bandolero, and lower-level stock car phenom. He was eighteen when he made his Xfinity debut at Dover, his Cup debut at Loudon, and his Camping World debut at Talladega, all in the summer of 2008. He ran the full Cup schedules and partial Xfinity schedules during his four years (2009–2012) in Toyotas at Joe Gibbs Racing.

Surprisingly, especially in light of what came later, his only Gibbs victories were Loudon in 2009 and Pocono in 2012. He consistently got poles, top fives, and top tens, but those two isolated victories and four seasons between sixteenth and twenty-fourth in points weren't exactly what NASCAR watchers expected. Compare that to his Xfinity record at Gibbs: twenty-two poles and eighteen victories in 110 starts.

In Cup, it may have been a matter of being overshadowed by veteran teammates Kyle Busch and Denny Hamlin. During their 144 starts together—thirty-six each for four seasons—Hamlin won eighteen races, Busch won twelve, and Logano won two. It was no great shock, then, when former champion Matt Kenseth replaced Logano after 2012 and promptly won seven times.

The Kenseth-to-Gibbs move left Roger Penske free to recruit Logano to his No. 22 team. Logano wasted no time in reminding critics that he was still "Sliced" after all. Since joining Team Penske in 2013, he's won seventeen poles and twenty-five races, including a Daytona 500, a full-distance victory at Loudon, three at Talladega, and three in Penske's backyard in Michigan. He was top ten in points eight of the last nine years after enduring four bad years at JGR. Among his three victories in 2018 was the championship finale at Homestead that gave Penske his second Cup Series title.

NASCAR veteran Mark Martin watched closely during Logano's teen years and was fully convinced he would be a superstar. He urged team owner Jack Roush to recruit him to no avail . . . which is how Logano ended up at Joe Gibbs Racing.

And the beat goes on. Logano has won six races and been a consistent frontrunner in his three seasons since winning the 2018 title. His Cup resume going into the 2022 season: twenty-two poles and twenty-seven victories in 471 starts, plus 138 top fives, and 240 top tens. Eight of his nine top-ten points finishes (in thirteen full seasons) have come with Penske.

CHAPTER 19

Terry Labonte

Darlington (SC) Raceway, Sept. 1, 1980

There were times when the motorsports media didn't know quite what to do with this new, young, soft-spoken stock car driver from Texas with the interesting last name.

"Terry" was the easy part. Your basic T-E-R-R-Y. But was it L-a-b-o-n-t-e? Or L-a-B-o-n-t-e? Or maybe L-'-B-o-n-t-e? Or even L-A-B-o-n-t-e? You would find it written—incorrectly, in many cases—all sorts of ways.

But any confusion began clearing on Labor Day weekend of 1978. That's when L-a-b-o-n-t-e, driving Billy Hagan's No. 92 Chevrolet, finished fourth in the iconic Southern 500 at Darlington Raceway in South Carolina. The three drivers ahead of him that day were pretty good racers: three-time champions Cale Yarborough and Darrell Waltrip, and seven-time champion Richard Petty, all of them future Hall of Famers.

That initial top-five finish was heady stuff for the twenty-one-year-old in his first Cup Series start. Not just his first Darlington start . . . his first Cup Series start *ANYWHERE*. Two seasons later—after fifty-eight more starts—Labonte drove a Hagan-owned car into victory lane at Darlington for the first of his twenty-two career victories.

Terry Labonte roared in from Texas to become a Cup champion.
DAVID GRIFFIN

"For some reason, Darlington was always good for me," said Labonte, long-retired after a thirty-seven-year career. "When Billy asked if I wanted to race at Darlington, I said I thought we were going to Martinsville and North Wilkesboro. You know, places like that. He said, 'We are . . . but we were going to Darlington, too.' So, I said, 'Oh . . . OK.' There wasn't a lot of discussion. I just remember thinking, 'At least I'm going to get to run one race.'"

Labonte had moved from Texas to North Carolina in 1978. He had grown up racing go-karts and quarter-midgets, including winning a quarter-midget national championship at nine. As a teenager, he and his crew chief/father, Bob Labonte, had advanced to short-track stock cars in the Houston area. Showing talent on both dirt and asphalt, between 1975 and 1977 Terry won weekly short-track championships in Corpus Christi, Houston, and San Antonio.

The next logical step was a move to stock car racing's heartland. The family moved to central North Carolina, where Terry became a crewman on Hagan's young-but-ambitious team featuring driver Skip Manning. When Hagan wanted a new driver, he stayed in-house and chose Labonte. In the weeks after his fourth place at Darlington, Labonte was seventh at Richmond, ninth at Martinsville, twenty-fourth at Charlotte, and thirteenth at Atlanta. (By running only five races, he retained his all-important rookie status for 1979.)

After some missteps with crew chief Darrell Bryant in 1978, Labonte began to shine in 1979 with thirteen top-ten finishes and a tenth-place finish in points. His first career victory came at Darlington in 1980, two years after making his impressive Cup debut there. He started tenth and led only the last two laps to beat David Pearson in a finish that fell his way in a most unusual fashion.

Labonte was a competitive fourth coming for the two-to-go flag when leader Pearson suddenly smacked the Turn Two wall. Second-running Dale Earnhardt also crashed even as third-running Benny Parsons spun to the Turn Two apron. Labonte steered through the chaos and passed the wounded Pearson just before the yellow and white flags. The official margin of victory was "under caution," but the real margin was perhaps half a fender.

"I didn't run through any oil or water or anything," Labonte said at the time. "Obviously, something happened to them [the front three] that didn't happen to me. I don't know . . . maybe I was in the wrong lane or something. I was wide-open when I caught Pearson exiting Turn Four coming for the flags. I don't think he ever saw me coming. The white and yellow were out, so I knew I had to pass him before the line. When we got there [running the bottom groove], I could tell I had beaten him. I couldn't believe it, that we had just won the Southern 500."

Labonte's two Cup Series championships spanned twelve years (1984–1996), a record for years between titles.

Labonte won six times with Hagan, four with Junior Johnson, and twelve with Rick Hendrick. (Two were in Fords with Johnson, one was in an Oldsmobile with Hagan, the others were in Chevrolets with Hagan and Hendrick.) His last full season was 2004 with Hendrick, but he didn't retire until after running ten partial seasons (2005–2014) with a dozen different owners. He ended his career on a zero for sixty-three slide, perhaps another case of a former star hanging on too long.

"He was a great racer, a money driver," said former crew chief Dale Inman, who led the team's 1984 Cup-winning effort. "When we got close for that championship, he knew how to win. He got hurt really bad at Riverside in the fall of 1982 [leg, ankle, severe facial injuries; eight days hospitalized] and it took him a while to get over it. But when he did—when he recovered and was right again—we really clicked. And he was good in those big-money all-star races and when the championship was close."

Ironically, the first and last of Labonte's twenty-two career Cup Series victories came exactly twenty-three years apart, at Darlington on Labor Day weekends of 1980 and 2003.

After his 1984 Cup win with Hagan and Inman, Labonte won the 1996 title with Hendrick and crew chief Gary DeHart. In addition to his Cup successes, Labonte won eleven Xfinity races and another in the Camping World series. And everything was spelled properly when he went into the NASCAR Hall of Fame in the Class of 2016 with Jerry Cook, Bruton Smith, Bobby Isaac, and Curtis Turner. Four years later Labonte was back in the Hall of Fame in Charlotte to officially introduce his brother, Bobby, as a member of the hall's Class of 2020.

Not surprisingly, Terry doesn't apologize for those last ten mediocre seasons. To many racing purists, those seasons represent an unsightly blot on the brilliant career of a two-time Cup Series champion. For some, it was difficult to watch.

"I was having fun and enjoying myself with those rides," he said. "I'd done full-season stuff long enough, but I didn't want to quit altogether. I found there's a whole world outside racing. A few races here and there was just what I wanted. I don't have any regrets at all."

CHAPTER 20

Kyle Petty

Richmond (VA) Raceway, Feb. 23, 1986

Kyle Petty was twenty-six-years-old and six winless seasons into his NASCAR career when he heard the words he'll remember forever: "I think we're leading! I think we're going to win this thing!"

They came from Eddie Wood of Wood Brothers Racing, the team's pit box spotter for the 1986 Miller High Life 400 at Richmond Raceway. And Wood was right: Petty, driving the team's No. 7 Ford (the unfamiliar number was a concession to its 7-Eleven store sponsorship), was indeed leading en route to his first NASCAR Cup Series victory.

Petty's response to Wood's message? "No [freaking] way, man."

In the season's second race, Petty was about to take the caution flag (this was before overtime rules were added) that would ensure the first of his eight career victories. He also won at Charlotte for the Woods and at Watkins Glen, Pocono, Dover, and three times at Rockingham for Felix Sabates.

It seemed appropriate that Petty should get his breakthrough victory at Richmond. His grandfather, Lee, had won there twice in the 1950s. His father, Richard, had won there *thirteen* times over four decades. And now Kyle, just four caution laps from his first victory in his 170th start.

Kyle Petty visited victory lane for the first time at Richmond Raceway in 1986. *BARB SAUNDERS / BRH RACING ARCHIVES*

To this day, the third-generation driver admits he was lucky. But he steadfastly clutches his family's long-held belief about racing: "The fans said we were lucky and the media said we were lucky . . . because we *were* lucky," the sixty-two-year-old TV commentator said. "But nobody within the four walls of the NASCAR garages said we were lucky because they've all been there. The scales of racing eventually even out. You get one here, you lose one there. It's happened to everybody at one time or another. That day, it was our turn; on another day, it won't be."

Other than his fondness for the half-mile, low-banked, outdated track, Petty didn't sense anything particularly favorable that weekend. "I remember we had good pizza the night before," he said blithely. "And I always enjoyed Richmond because Richmond and Martinsville were big Petty tracks. Those people up there loved them some Richard Petty. It was a nice day and I had a great ride with the Woods, so I remember it felt like it might be good. Nothing specific, but an overall feeling that we might do pretty well."

Petty, competitive from the start, approached the final laps running fifth. He would have been ecstatic with that since most of his other 169 starts had been on longer, faster tracks; only a few dozen had been on short tracks. All of which led him to quip later: "Who would have ever envisioned me winning on a short track? It was like throwing me in the ocean and telling me to get back to shore."

Fortunes changed abruptly down the stretch. With three laps remaining, second-running Dale Earnhardt hooked the right-rear of leader Darrell Waltrip, sending him into the railing between Turns Three and Four. Third- and fourth-place Joe Ruttman and Geoffrey Bodine were too close to avoid the scene. Finally, the lapped cars of Trevor Boys and Buddy Arrington were involved and almost blocked the track.

Petty leads one of the most successful charity efforts in NASCAR history. Kyle Petty's Charity Ride Across America, a motorcycle ride that includes dozens of riders and raises funds for Victory Junction Camp, the Petty family's North Carolina camp for children with chronic illnesses. The ride is in its third decade.

Meanwhile, back in Turns One and Two: "I looked across the infield and saw them wrecking," Petty said years later. "That's how far behind I was, fifth-place by half a track. I went down the backstretch and saw people slowing down for the yellow lights. At that point, I wasn't sure if they were lapped cars or not. I slowed and geared down, and picked my way through [Turns] Three and Four. Man, there was carnage everywhere.

"I was running really slow when I went by the wreck, then went back up through the gears to take the yellow. That's when Eddie came on the radio and said he thought we were leading and were going to win. I couldn't hardly believe it because I didn't know which cars ahead of

Kyle Petty carried
the Petty family's
racing success into
a third generation.
DICK CONWAY

me were lapped or truthfully ahead of me. We were the first lead-lap car to the line for the yellow and checkered, so I'll never apologize for winning like that."

Richmond didn't have a huge outdoor TV screen, so none of the Woods could see the accident from pit road. But the reaction of fans across from them in the Turns Three and Four bleachers let them know something big had happened. "I didn't say anything to Kyle on the radio until he came through [Turn] Four, ahead of everybody else," Wood recalled. "I didn't know he was leading until I saw him come around the corner. That's when I said I thought he was leading and we were going to win. We were lucky, but we'd been pretty good all day. We were going to finish good, anyway."

Petty was the third driver to get his breakthrough victory with the Woods. Team founder Glen Wood was first in 1960, followed by Tiny Lund in 1963, Kyle in 1986, Dale Jarrett in 1991, Elliott Sadler in 2001, Trevor Bayne in 2011, and Ryan Blaney in 2017. All told, seventeen drivers have contributed to the family-owned team's ninety-nine victories.

None could have been happier than Kyle, whose job to continue the Petty family legacy must have occasionally felt overwhelming. "Let me tell you, man," he said, "that was a big day for both families. No doubt, after everybody they'd had ahead of me [David Pearson, Neil Bonnett, and Buddy Baker], I was surely a step down. So, that was a big win for the Woods, big for me, and big for my family. It was a [financially helpful] Winners Circle win. And it was good for the sponsors [7-Eleven and CITGO].

"Daddy didn't come to victory lane or the hauler, but I'm sure I ran into him somewhere later that afternoon. We were never real touchy-feely kind of racers. We were always *expected* to win, *expected* to do our jobs and win without a lot of emotion. But I know he was happy and proud, and my mother was, too. No matter how we got there, winning Richmond was a big day for the Pettys and the Woods."

CHAPTER 21

Donnie Allison

North Carolina Motor Speedway, June 16, 1968

D onnie Allison will be remembered mostly for a race he didn't win. And that's unfortunate. Allison had a more-than-respectable racing career, following his brother, Bobby, into the big time after short-track success and winning ten NASCAR Cup races. He won at Daytona Beach, Talladega, Charlotte, and Bristol. He won at Atlanta after one of the sport's craziest scoring controversies. He drove in the Indianapolis 500 and finished fourth at racing's most famous track as a rookie.

But Allison's career forever will be linked to the 1979 Daytona 500 and its finish, one that has been repeated a bajillion times in video replays and in still photographs. For the three or four people who might not have heard, that race ended with Allison and Cale Yarborough crashing in the third turn while battling for the lead on the last lap. The pair continued that confrontation in the infield, along with Bobby Allison. It was a fight seen 'round the world, thanks to the cameras of CBS.

Richard Petty happily inherited the race lead and the win as the Allisons and Yarborough wrestled on Daytona's infield sod. Donnie and Cale were left to explain the finish over and over and over again, even in their senior years. They long ago made up, but each will tell you he really should have won stock car racing's biggest event.

Donnie Allison ended his Cup career with ten wins, the first coming at Rockingham, North Carolina, in 1968. *BILL NIVEN / BRH RACING ARCHIVES*

Allison scored his first Cup victory in 1968 at North Carolina Motor Speedway in Rockingham. He had threatened to win in the previous months, finishing third at Atlanta, third at Martinsville, and second at Charlotte.

The Rockingham race was scheduled March 10 but was rained out and rescheduled June 16, which turned out to be a brutally hot day in the North Carolina Sandhills. Five-hundred-lap marathons at the one-mile track were tough under normal circumstances, but the mid-June heat added to the stress.

Allison crashed his car, owned by A. J. Foyt, in practice leading to the 1970 Indy 500, a race in which Allison finished fourth. At Christmas that year, Allison received a "present" from Foyt—a shipment containing some of the pieces of the wrecked car. The package arrived COD (cash on delivery).

"It was a typical Rockingham race where different guys led," Allison remembered. "I was in a race with somebody all day, be it Bobby or Richard or Cale or whoever. In the end, I felt like it proved the fact that I could drive a race car. Ralph Moody [owner/mechanic] had been telling the Ford people that for two years. He really helped me, really was persistent."

Allison led 154 laps, including the final 129. He was more than two laps in front of brother Bobby, who finished second, at the checkered flag. The race lasted five hours and two minutes, a length not unusual in those days of 500-mile races at one-mile tracks.

"It was tough," Allison said. "These guys run a 500-mile race now and jump out of the car and jump on it and all. In those days, they had to get us out of the car with a damn crane."

In other words, it was a long day.

Allison won in a Banjo Matthews–prepared car. Matthews was a NASCAR pioneer and is recognized as one of the sport's all-time leading car builders.

"Banjo was not just smart in mechanical stuff; he was a good coach," Allison said. "He knew what it took. He never once tried to boss me around. At Daytona and Talladega, every time he walked by me, he would say, 'Can you hold it wide open?' And I better not stutter. I better say yes."

Allison won the 1970 Firecracker 400 at Daytona International Speedway in a Matthews car. "They gave the winner a boat, a camper, and a Rolex watch," Allison said. "I remember Banjo asking me in

One of Allison's most emotional moments in racing occurred on a day in which he didn't compete. Two weeks after the death of his nephew, star driver Davey Allison, in July 1993, Allison celebrated Davey's life by driving one of Davey's No. 28 Fords around Talladega Superspeedway as part of pre-race ceremonies. He traveled the 2.66 miles with tears streaming down his face. "I almost didn't make it through that," he said later.

victory lane which one I wanted. I said, 'I'm going to get them all.' He said, 'No, you're not.' Well, I got all of them. I gave the boat to my father and the watch to my oldest son. The camper—I don't know where it is."

Allison's career took a bad turn in 1981 when he was seriously injured in a crash during the World 600 at Charlotte. His car hit the outside wall, dropped across the racetrack, and was hit by Dick Brooks's following car. Allison suffered a broken left leg, a broken cheekbone, a fractured shoulder blade, several broken ribs, and a damaged lung. He recovered to race again but never returned to victory lane.

His last win occurred under a cloud of controversy in the Dixie 500 at Atlanta in 1978. Allison finished the race three car lengths in front of Richard Petty, but, after a recheck of scorecards, NASCAR declared Petty the winner. Allison and his car owner, Hoss Ellington, continued to press their case, and another scorecard check revealed that a scorer had missed one of Allison's laps. Three hours and ten minutes after the race ended, NASCAR reversed its position and gave the win to Allison, who left the track before learning of his victory.

NASCAR President Bill France Jr. called the situation "an all-time NASCAR screw-up on scoring."

It was Allison's final checkered flag.

CHAPTER 22

Buddy Baker

Charlotte (NC) Motor Speedway, Oct. 15, 1967

Before and after his retirement as a NASCAR driver, Buddy Baker
served as a consultant and coach for up-and-coming racers. Ryan
Newman is perhaps his most famous pupil.

There was a time, however, when Baker was the student and others
did the teaching. Although he was the son of Hall of Fame driver Buck
Baker, Buddy needed help as he entered the sport where his father had
been a dominant force.

In the early years of his career, Baker approached pioneer driver
Curtis Turner for advice in negotiating the very difficult Occoneechee
Speedway, a fast 0.9-mile dirt track in Hillsborough, North Carolina.

"I asked him where he backed off going into the corner," Baker
remembered years later. "He told me, and when I got to that point I
might as well have kept it wide open. I wasn't going to make it through
the corner anyway. I went backward through the gate and into the parking lot. I came back in and said, 'Hey, are you sure you drive it in that
deep?' He said, 'Yeah, but I've got twenty years' experience.'"

Baker did two things very well—drive race cars really fast and tell
stories. His gifts as a storyteller served him well when he finally moved

Buddy Baker, shown here at Martinsville Speedway, was known as the Gentle Giant, but he was famously fast on NASCAR's biggest tracks. *DICK CONWAY*

away from driving and built a second career in motorsports television and radio.

Baker loved to tell the story of a long-ago race at a Tennessee short track. He was injured in a crash. He was loaded into the rear of an ambulance. When the ambulance left the scene with a bolt, Baker left the ambulance. His gurney rolled out the back of the open door.

Elzie Wylie Baker Jr. (nobody called him that) began his Cup career in 1959 but rarely raced a full-season schedule. He was most at home on the circuit's fastest tracks; six of his nineteen career Cup wins were scored at Daytona International Speedway and Talladega Superspeedway.

Baker recorded a bit of NASCAR history March 24, 1970, when he became the first stock car driver to average more than 200 miles per hour in a lap around a closed course. Baker reached that speed—200.096 mph—at Talladega Superspeedway, then in its second year, during test runs. He drove a winged Dodge Daytona, one of the fastest cars of that—or any—era.

"It's the most wonderful feeling I've had in a long, long time," Baker said afterward. "I'm tickled to death."

Three years earlier, Baker had scored his first Cup victory, leading the final seventy-eight laps on the way to victory in the National 500 at Charlotte Motor Speedway. Baker, in a Ray Fox Dodge, outran second-place Bobby Isaac by one-lap-plus. Baker called it "the greatest day of my life." His win was noteworthy beyond it being his first. Richard Petty started the race with a streak of ten straight wins and finally saw his near-complete domination of the tour halted.

Although Baker celebrated his first victory with numerous adjectives, he often told friends that nothing could top his win in the 1980 Daytona 500. Driving a car nicknamed the Gray Ghost because of its black-and-gray paint scheme, one that made his approaching car almost invisible to competitors, he won the race with a stunning average speed of 177.602 miles per hour. That speed remains a 500 record.

Baker said he grew up racing against men he called his heroes.

"The first time I beat them I realized you're not really beating them, you're beating the day or the situation," he said. "Then you say, hey, maybe I'll make it now. But every time you get a little overconfident like that, you get knocked back about fifty feet.

"The first thing the veterans told me is that it's impossible, that you'll never beat us. And by the time you get good enough to beat us we'll be retired anyhow. I remember them asking me, 'Have you shaved yet?' or 'Are you still on milk or have you gone to a grown-up drink yet?'"

Baker began his career driving his father Buck's cars. Much later, they teamed up again in operating the Buck Baker Driving School, a school for new and aspiring racers, at North Carolina Motor Speedway.

Baker did grow up—at six-five he was one of the tallest drivers in motorsports. And one of the most nervous. He was particularly nervous before qualifying. Amused garage area workers would watch as he paced up and down the garage waiting for his turn on track. A newspaper once asked him to wear a pedometer on qualifying day to record how many miles he walked in a nervous pace, but he grew tired of the experiment and removed the device before jumping in his car.

What Baker might have called a "lowlight" of his career occurred at Texas World Speedway, where he had a two-lap lead on the field but lost concentration and ran into the rear of another car during a caution period, losing a shot at victory.

"Buddy was always wide open, and that's the way he raced and lived his life," said Petty, whose team employed Baker as a driver in the 1970s. "He was always full of energy. He was a person you wanted to be around because he always made you feel better. He raced with us, shared his stories with us, and became our friend."

Baker, a native of Charlotte, North Carolina, died in 2015 at the age of seventy-four.

CHAPTER 23

Wendell Scott

Jacksonville (FL) Speedway Park, Dec. 1, 1963

While it's true the late Wendell Scott wasn't a bootlegger by trade, it's also true that shortly after World War II he often hauled moonshine to help support his real job . . . racing NASCAR stock cars.

In addition to running an auto repair shop and driving a taxi, the Danville, Virginia, native sought his fame and fortune on short, bumpy, dusty speedways throughout the Southeast. Bootlegging might have brought money into the Scott household, but it was outrunning the white good ol' boys that obsessed the former motor pool corporal in General George S. Patton's "Big Red One" during his three years with the US Army in Europe.

Scott's illegal sideline gave him a well-earned reputation as a talented wheelman. The Danville police often closed in, but never got close enough to catch him hauling a load. He was smart enough and fast enough and creative enough to almost always escape. Both the locals and the feds grudgingly respected him for being so good at what he did. Besides, he never put himself, his frustrated pursuers, or his customers in danger during his deliveries.

In the early 1950s, the promoter of the Danville Fairgrounds Speedway approached police with an unusual request: "Help us find a Black

Wendell Scott during a pit stop at Augusta Speedway in November of 1965. *JERRY OVERMAN / SMYLE MEDIA*

man who can drive a race car well enough to attract Black fans to our track." Not surprisingly, the police directed them to Scott's modest home, where he maintained his 'shine cars and cabs, and sometimes worked on cars for customers.

Within weeks he was racing at the local weekly track, doing well enough to make money. He began winning fairly often, building his name and making ends meet by nursing his hand-me-down equipment and saving every spare dime. Despite facing blatant racism and bigotry on the road, Scott never considered quitting. He did well enough in Virginia and surrounding states to reach NASCAR's prestigious Cup Series early in 1961. He raced full time from then until retiring in 1973 after an accident at the Talladega Superspeedway in Alabama left him financially ruined and badly injured.

His lone Cup victory in 495 starts was as notable for what happened *after* the checkered flag as for what had happened *before.*

The historic victory came in December of 1963 on the dirty, dusty, rutted, half-mile bullring called Jacksonville Speedway Park in northeast Florida. Scott was forty-two years old and four years into a career that produced a 113-race losing streak. He was seldom a frontrunner but never a quitter, admired and respected for being the only Black racer in what was overwhelmingly a white man's sport. Some of the bigotry and hostility so disturbing early on was slowly fading in a few places, but not in Jacksonville.

Scott started fifteenth on the twenty-two-car grid for the two-hundred-lap, one-hundred-mile race. He was considered little more than a "field-filler," a veteran backmarker given little to no chance of winning. Pole-winner Jack Smith, Ned Jarrett, and Richard Petty swapped the lead until Petty slowed abruptly at lap 175 with an ailing engine.

Scott had run well enough to be scored the leader when Petty dropped out. He cleanly inherited the lead at that point—there was never any doubt about that, but inexplicably was scored third at the checkered flag, behind apparent winner Buck Baker and runner-up Smith. Upset but patient, Scott requested a scoring review, a perfectly understandable reaction and not an uncommon request at a time when scoring errors were common.

As the review dragged into the evening, Scott and his family recognized the truth: officials didn't want him celebrating his first-ever NASCAR victory at their track. They couldn't stomach the visual of a forty-two-year-old Black man from Virginia posing beside the young, attractive, white race queen holding the winner's trophy. One of her traditional duties, of course, was to kiss the winner while photographers flashed away, preserving the historic moment. The Scotts have never doubted why their father/grandfather was treated that way.

Officials eventually admitted that the scoring was flawed, that Scott had actually lapped Baker twice, running two laps more than required.

> **The NASCAR Hall of Fame is one of several Halls to honor Scott. Also: Motorsports Hall of Fame of America, Virginia Sports Hall of Fame, Virginia Motorsports Hall of Fame, National Motorsports Press Association Hall of Fame, and International Motorsports Hall of Fame.**

By the time the two-lap error was corrected and Scott was declared the winner, most fans, the media, and other teams had long since left for home, unaware that Scott had been ruled the winner. The track was virtually deserted when Scott got his $1,000 winner's check and headed back toward Danville.

But the story doesn't end there. Even before the correct result was certified, Baker and his team were northbound toward their Charlotte shop. They apparently took the winner's trophy, which officials gave Baker in victory lane. To its consternation, the No. 34 Ford team never got its rightful trophy. In his later years, Scott said the missing trophy meant as much as the $1,000 check. (Baker's survivors have said they have no knowledge of the missing trophy.)

In 2010, two racing fan clubs in the Southeast gave Scott's children a replica of the trophy their father never got. That helped ease some pain, but not much. In 2021, eldest son Frank Scott asked NASCAR to step forward and make a public gesture with yet another replica trophy.

"NASCAR had nothing to do with the replica trophy the racing club gave us ten years ago," he said. "We'd like for NASCAR to have an official ceremony for maybe ten minutes next year and give us a trophy of their own. There's your easy fix right there; that would make it right. And let me tell you: with everything going on right now, that little ceremony would help them as much as it would help us."

And so it was that in late summer of 2021, in a pre-race ceremony at Daytona International Speedway, NASCAR presented Scott family members with another replica of the 1963 trophy that remains lost. It fulfilled one of Wendell Scott's predictions, made shortly before he died in 1990: "I may not be with you at the time, but someday I'll get that trophy," he had said. "Just because I might lose the race doesn't mean I'm defeated."

Richard Pryor portrayed Scott in the 1977 movie "Greased Lightning," which also starred Cleavon Little, Pam Grier, Vincent Gardenia, and noted civil rights activist Julian Bond.

CHAPTER 24

Darrell Waltrip

Nashville (TN) Speedway, May 10, 1975

Any ranking of NASCAR's most important figures since its 1948 founding must feature Bill France and his son, Bill Jr., near the top. Seven-time champions Richard Petty and Dale Earnhardt will be there, too. And despite never turning a lap, R. J. Reynolds Tobacco Co. executive Ralph Seagraves gets a spot.

Then, somewhere else near the top is ol' D. W.

Yes, three-time champion and eighty-four-time winner Darrell Waltrip might have been the man who changed NASCAR Cup Series racing more than anyone. He didn't win the most poles, races, or Cups, but his talent, showmanship, and PR savvy forced the sport to upgrade itself going into the "modern era."

It's likely that NASCAR changed enormously after Waltrip arrived in the early 1970s. At twenty-five, the Kentucky native carried the unmistakable aura of a superstar-in-waiting. He was an enormous talent who almost immediately became NASCAR's most polarizing figure. He was cocky and often irritating, but defended himself with Dizzy Dean's mantra, "If you can do it, it ain't bragging."

Nobody in the Cup garage was as outspoken as the man Cale Yarborough once called "Jaws." Certainly, nobody toyed with the media

Young and brash, Darrell Waltrip was a transformative figure in stock car racing. *Dick Conway*

and used it so skillfully. He was undeniably gifted, as good at getting in your head as beating you to the flag. Granted, NASCAR had plenty of huge talents, but nobody had arrived as its first "full package."

Listen to what industry insiders said about Waltrip:

"How important was he?" said retired Charlotte Motor Speedway (CMS) promoter Humpy Wheeler. "Man, he was *very* important; maybe the most important driver we've ever had. We needed a new superstar back then, somebody who could get racing on Page 1. There might not be anything going on, then here comes Darrell, saying stuff that got everybody's attention. He was like Muhammad Ali . . . always talking and stirring the pot.

"He was exactly what we needed—a half-good guy and a half-villain who moved the needle. It's funny about drivers: they want to get along; they want to like each other. Well, Darrell didn't care about that. He'd tick you off and the media would run with it. I can tell you from experience he helped me sell a bunch of tickets."

Eddie Gossage worked with Wheeler at CMS, learning racing PR at the knee of the master. Not surprisingly, his view of Waltrip's importance is similar to his old boss's.

"There's no question he may have been the most transformative driver of them all," says Gossage, former president of Texas Motor Speedway. "He helped move the sport from backyard mechanics to people who looked and talked like he did. He didn't fit the mold, so he was better at advancing the sport than anybody. And he was a smart-ass when nobody else was a smart-ass; he walked the walk and talked the talk. That's why so many people didn't always like him."

When Waltrip retired in 2000 and went into TV, his twenty-nine-year resume showed fifty-nine poles, eighty-four victories, three Cup championships, eighteen top-ten points seasons, and a Most Popular

A high school track star, Darrell Waltrip didn't slow down when he moved into Cup racing from Tennessee short tracks.
DICK CONWAY

Darrell Waltrip powers one of his first Cup cars around Martinsville Speedway. *Dick Conway*

Driver award. He went into the NASCAR Hall of Fame in 2012 and has been inducted into upwards of a half dozen others. There's almost nothing he hasn't done.

Ironically, he's now revered as one of racing's grand old men, a respected figure whose opinions are still valued in Daytona Beach and Charlotte. Dare we say it: he's now accepted by many who once booed him at every turn. "My glory days may have passed," Waltrip said late in his career, "but at least I had glory days."

Waltrip and crew chief Jake Elder debuted with five Cup races in 1972 in Waltrip's hand-me-down No. 95 Mercury. They did nineteen more starts in 1973 and another sixteen in 1974. By the time they went full time in 1975, they already had a pole, nine top-fives, and nineteen top-tens in forty starts. Not bad

Waltrip's fifteen-year winning streak ended in 1990, when Brett Bodine beat him at North Wilkesboro Speedway. To this day, Waltrip is convinced NASCAR scoring and timing had it wrong, that he beat Bodine.

Darrell Waltrip won races for the DiGard team before moving on to score championships with team owner Junior Johnson.
DICK CONWAY

for a relatively inexperienced kid driving less-than-competitive equipment on a relatively modest budget.

Almost predictably, his first Cup victory came on the half-mile Nashville Fairgrounds Speedway. "I knew I had a slight advantage anytime I raced there," Waltrip acknowledged. "That's where I grew up racing, so I knew that track better than any other. I figured if I couldn't win there, I might not be able to win anywhere."

Waltrip had won upwards of sixty times at Nashville during his pre-Cup career. They included several dozen ARCA, ASA, USAC, Late Model, and Sportsman races. Afterward, during his NASCAR days, he won an Xfinity race and eight Cup races there. The first of those eight Cup victories—and the first of his eighty-four—came on May 10, 1975, in the Music City 420.

Waltrip won the pole and led the first forty-seven laps before third-starting Yarborough led 48–320. But that overwhelming performance ended at lap 321 with a blown engine in Yarborough's No. 11 Chevrolet. Waltrip inherited the point and easily stayed ahead the final one hundred laps, beating Benny Parsons by two laps.

"I was good that night," Waltrip recalled. "I wasn't as good as Cale and [owner] Junior Johnson, but I was good enough to win the race. And, you know, I always knew Nashville would be where I'd win my first one. I knew I was a good driver; the deal was for me to get the car as good as the driver. It took a while because at first we didn't have the money to get the car to the driver's level."

To Waltrip, the Nashville victory "broke the ice" and opened the door to what would become a marvelous career. He won at least once a year for the next fourteen years, missing only in 1990. At the height of his career—twelve victories each in 1981 and 1982—he was winning about once every three weeks with Junior Johnson. But he tailed off late, going zero for twenty-three in 1990, then winning only twice in 1991, and three times in 1992. He endured a zero for 251 tailspin the last eight years of his career.

Sigh: even the great ones sometimes stay too long.

When he quit racing after 2000, Waltrip went directly to broadcasting on FOX TV as its first "driver talent." By the time he left the booth after 2020, Waltrip had worked approximately 330 races and 1,500 practice and qualifying sessions for the network.

CHAPTER 25

Kevin Harvick

Atlanta (GA) Motor Speedway, Mar. 11, 2001

The death of Dale Earnhardt in the 2001 Daytona 500 left a gaping hole in NASCAR racing in general and Richard Childress Racing (RCR) in particular. While nobody could fill the seven-time Cup Series champion's shoes, Kevin Harvick did a creditable job of helping RCR maintain relevance as one of the sport's best organizations.

The 2001 spring race at Atlanta Motor Speedway was the first step in that direction.

It was March 11 when Harvick, a young, aggressive driver from California, won the Cracker Barrel 500. Crewmen from RCR began embracing anyone in sight, weeping unashamedly on pit road, and pointing skyward with thanks to God. Everything seemed familiar . . . yet at the same time everything seemed so different.

Three weeks earlier, at Daytona International Speedway, those same crewmen had hugged and cried . . . this time after learning that Earnhardt had died in a last-lap crash. If the 1959 plane crash that took Buddy Holly, the Big Bopper, and Richie Valens was called "the day the music died," then February 18, 2001, was generally considered the day NASCAR died.

Kevin Harvick edged Jeff Gordon by 0.006 of a second at Atlanta Motor Speedway to notch his first win.
NIGEL KINRADE

For millions of fans, Harvick's photo-finish victory over Jeff Gordon at Atlanta—the first of his career—may have started bringing NASCAR back to life.

"Winning Atlanta did as much for the whole sport as for anything else," team owner Richard Childress said of that day more than twenty-one years ago. "To see us go out and win in Dale's car [renumbered from 3 to 29] was emotional for all of us, but it was good. It was just what all of us needed. There have been only a few moments in the sport that have given everybody a better feeling about what was going on. Kevin winning at Atlanta was one of them.

"It showed that Richard Childress Racing was still out here, still racing hard, and still winning. I think that was important for the whole sport. Then, Dale Jr. coming back to win [in Daytona Beach] in July was another of those moments. And when he came back in February of the next year to win the Xfinity race in the 3 car [at Daytona] was another one. They were all big moments for the sport, not just for our team and for DEI [Dale Earnhardt Inc.]."

Harvick is among six drivers with Cup and Xfinity titles, along with Bobby Labonte, Chase Elliott, Kyle Busch, Martin Truex Jr., and Brad Keselowski.

Few would have picked Harvick to help stock car racing heal from one of its deepest wounds. He had endured a short and undistinguished Camping World Truck Series career between 1995 and 2000. He'd started by driving for his family-owned team, then for owners Wayne Spears and Jim Herrick. In 2000, Childress recruited him as a "project driver," beginning in the Xfinity Series and working toward a Cup career beside Earnhardt. Based on three victories and third in points, he easily won the 2000 Xfinity Rookie of the Year award. He was scheduled to return to that series in 2001 before going full-time Cup racing in 2002.

Everything changed when Earnhardt died.

Suddenly, instead of running the full 2001 Xfinity schedule with an occasional Cup race thrown in, Harvick was promoted to run not only the full Xfinity schedule but also the remaining thirty-five Cup races as well. His daunting two-series, full-season grind began at Rockingham, North Carolina, the weekend after Earnhardt died. Suddenly, private jets, helicopters, and shuttle vehicles were put on standby for RCR's use.

Other drivers had run both series at the same time, but nobody had ever replaced an iconic motorsports legend in the process. Three weekends into that cobbled-together plan, Harvick breathed new life into a still-grieving NASCAR community.

He started fifth for the 325-lap, five-hundred-mile race at the mile-and-a-half track south of Atlanta. With Kevin Hamlin as crew chief, Harvick led twelve laps early, stayed in serious contention all day, then led the last six. Jeff Gordon made a late-race, low-side charge in the waning laps, but came up short by 0.006 seconds. (It was almost too close to call from pit road, but indisputable upon further review.) After an impressive and well-received frontstretch burnout, Harvick did an emotional victory lap with his left hand out the window, showing three fingers.

Tears all around, from pit road to the NASCAR suites above the grandstands. Are you kidding me? Did you see what that kid just did?

At the time, Harvick didn't realize what his victory meant to motorsports in general. "I think it gave Dale's fans a reason to smile for the first time since his accident," Childress said many years later. "I know it lifted up everybody who worked at RCR. It was one of the greatest days in our company's history."

Harvick recently recalled that the importance of that victory didn't sink in for quite a while. "It took a couple of years because of everything going on at the time," the 2014 Cup Series champion said. "It took time to understand the situation [being in Cup so soon] and the magnitude of the situation with me replacing Dale. They were very confusing moments, and it was hard to wrap my arms around the magnitude of that win."

Even though he's won most of NASCAR's showcase events, nothing in his mind will overshadow that Atlanta victory. "There won't be a

Kevin Harvick replaced Dale Earnhardt Sr. after Earnhardt's death at Daytona International Speedway. *DAVID GRIFFIN*

moment that matches that one in my career," he said. "It took time to appreciate how important it was to the company, how important it was to keeping RCR going. It wasn't important just for RCR, but for the sport in general."

He stayed with the No. 29 Chevrolet team from 2000 to 2013, winning twenty-three Cup races, forty Xfinity races, two Xfinity titles, and finishing nine times among the top ten in Cup points. He joined Stewart-Haas Racing in 2014 and immediately won the Cup title for teammate/co-owner Tony Stewart and co-owner Gene Haas. Going into the 2022 season he'd won an additional thirty-five Cup races for S-HR and had seven more top-ten points seasons. With 119 victories and three titles over three series—and despite his ofttime boorish behavior, he's a virtual cinch to eventually reach the NASCAR Hall of Fame.

To some fans, winning at Atlanta in March of 2001 would have been enough.

CHAPTER 26

Dale Earnhardt Jr.

Texas Motor Speedway, Apr. 2, 2000

I t can be argued that few drivers ever reached the top of any major American motorsports series carrying the weighty expectations that Dale Earnhardt Jr. carried into NASCAR's Cup Series in 1999.

By the time he arrived as a twenty-four-year-old rookie, his famous father had already won seventy-six races and seven championships. "Big Dale" was NASCAR's most popular driver (despite what Bill Elliott's fans said) and stood among the most influential figures in stock car racing. Junior was close by most of those years, watching, listening, and learning.

Factor in two Xfinity Series titles and you might appreciate the "expectation burden" Earnhardt Jr. brought along into Cup. After all, how do you follow "The Man in Black" and "The Intimidator"? Indeed, how do you follow your larger-than-life father?

Actually, Earnhardt Jr. handled everything pretty well. Still is, in fact.

The first of his twenty-six Cup Series victories came in his twelfth start, his first at Texas Motor Speedway. He and crew chief Tony Eury Sr. had struggled during their 1999 "getting ready" season: sixteenth at Charlotte, forty-third at Loudon, twenty-fourth at Michigan, tenth at Richmond, and fourteenth at Atlanta. They'd led one lap at Atlanta, but didn't have any lead-lap finishes during that introductory season.

Dale Earnhardt Jr. sparked a big celebration with his first win at Texas Motor Speedway in 2000.
DAVID GRIFFIN

The early months of 2000 weren't much better. Their No. 8 Chevrolet from Dale Earnhardt Inc. opened with thirteenth- and nineteenth-place finishes at Daytona Beach and Rockingham. They were tenth at Las Vegas, but struggled to twenty-ninth at Atlanta before crash-related finishes of fortieth at Darlington and thirty-eighth at Bristol. Hardly anyone anticipated anything special from them when NASCAR gathered for the Direct TV 500 in Fort Worth on April 2, 2000.

Fans—and perhaps the sport itself—got far more than they expected. Junior qualified fourth and led six times for 106 of the 334 laps, including the final fifty-three. His first career victory came a fairly comfortable 5.92 seconds ahead of Jeff Burton. He became NASCAR's latest first-time Cup winner since Tony Stewart in Richmond the previous fall.

In truth, it wasn't a particularly compelling race; the outcome never seemed in doubt. "It was pretty straightforward," the twenty-five-year-old fan favorite said at the time. "I had the flu most of that week, but that didn't bother me once we got going. There weren't any omens or superstitious feelings or signals. The car was good all day. Really, nothing too unusual happened. I pretty much did whatever I wanted in the car."

The victory helped convince him that just maybe he could be a full-time racer, after all. Until Texas—and despite all his success in Late Model stock cars and the Xfinity Series—he often doubted himself. He was well aware that the world was full of skillful Truck and Xfinity drivers who never found success at the next level. Too, he was young and professionally insecure and uncomfortable in social situations.

Junior is a long-time fan of the Washington Commanders (formerly Redskins) team and is a texting buddy with Coach Ron Rivera.

"To win at Cup took a huge weight off my shoulders," he said years later. "You never know what you can do until you actually do it. Everything that had come before in Xfinity didn't prove anything about winning in Cup. That was the best thing about that first one . . . the fact I had proved to myself and to my dad that I might be able to make a living racing. Texas helped lift that uncertainty."

Victory lane was pure chaos, but who cared? After finishing seventh, Dale Sr. parked his black No. 3 Chevrolet nearby and rushed to greet his son. "He kept yelling, 'Get out of there boy; get out of that car,' " Junior recalled. "I got out and climbed up on the roof, pretty excited. He helped pull me down . . . gave me a big hug and told me he loved me. He was pretty excited. It was a special moment because that was the hardest I'd ever drove a race car."

Earnhardt Sr. had plenty to say about his kid's first victory. "This is great [because] he worked hard," the seven-time champion said afterward. "It took a lot of hard work, and I knew it would be just a matter of time before he would win. The crew gave him a great car and he drove the hell out of it. He's something else, man."

CBS TV commentator Ned Jarrett had never seen the elder Earnhardt so excited. "Maybe when he won the Daytona 500 [in 1998]," Jarrett said. "But I don't know. Maybe not even then. It's a close call."

Junior's second victory came four races later, in May at Richmond Raceway. He started fifth, led only the final thirty-one of four hundred laps (he passed his father near the end), and won by 0.159 seconds over Terry Labonte. At the time, it looked like he was headed for long-term stardom similar to his father's.

The Earnhardts raced against each other only forty times in Cup: five times in 1999, thirty-four times in 2000, and the final time in the 2001 Daytona 500.

Already enormously popular, he won at least once a year for the family team— seventeen times in all—between 2000 and 2006. He left for Hendrick Motorsports after a winless 2007, determined to distance himself from his stepmother, Teresa. Most insiders knew he was tired of squabbling with her even as DEI's best days were slipping away. He won for Hendrick at Michigan that year, then added only eight more victories to his resume over the next nine seasons.

He retired after 2017, unwilling to risk more injuries after several accident-related concussions. He was a newlywed with an infant daughter (he now has two), financially secure for several lifetimes, and healthy for the first time in years. Today, he's the successful owner of a championship-caliber Xfinity Series company, a multilayered media personality, an articulate and insightful television commentator, and still as genuinely humble and popular as ever.

To the surprise of absolutely nobody, he was selected to the NASCAR Hall of Fame the instant he became eligible in 2020. He was uproariously welcomed to the hall in January of 2022, and his acceptance speech was considered one of the best in years.

As usual . . . once again exceeding expectations.

CHAPTER 27

Bill Elliott

Riverside (CA) Raceway, Nov. 20, 1983

W hen Bill Elliott finally ended a long drought and joined the ranks of NASCAR Cup race winners, it happened under unlikely circumstances and in an unlikely place.

Elliott had charged out of the north Georgia mountains to challenge the stars of NASCAR. He drove fast and talked slow, his Georgia drawl so pronounced that some interviewers strained to understand what he was saying. He did most of his talking on the track.

Elliott made his Cup debut in 1976 at Rockingham, North Carolina, driving a Ford entered by his family-owned team. He ran only thirty-two laps, parking with oil pump issues.

Leap forward seven years later, and Elliott has run 114 Cup races with the same number—"0"—in his win column. It is the final race of the 1983 season, and Elliott has made the cross-country trip to Riverside (California) International Raceway's road course. A short-track asphalt star before he jumped into Cup racing, Elliott has no particular love for road racing and, with no wins, starts the Winston Western 500 as an outlier of sorts.

That would change in the rain of that California afternoon. A second-place finisher eight times, Elliott finally would cross over into victory lane.

Bill Elliott talked slow but drove fast, eventually building a Hall of Fame career in NASCAR. *Dick Conway*

Tim Richmond and Darrell Waltrip were racing for the lead with seven laps to go when they crashed together in Turn Nine as rain began to fall. Richmond and Waltrip regained control of their cars, but their spins allowed Benny Parsons to take the lead, and Elliott followed him into second.

Weather put the field under caution temporarily, but the race returned to green conditions with five laps remaining. Elliott wasted no time. He zipped past Parsons at the first opportunity and sprinted into a comfortable lead. A few minutes later, harder rain fell, producing another caution. It quickly became clear that the race couldn't be restarted, and Elliott was home free, rolling into victory lane as rain pelted the track.

It was late November. Christmas would be a big one that year in the Elliott family.

"I can't believe it; I just can't believe it," Elliott said. "Everything went so wrong this year. Everything went so right today."

He had to attempt the winning pass quickly, Elliott said, because weather was threatening and opportunities were disappearing.

"I knew I had one chance to do it," he said. "I drove it down in there. Me and Benny got together, but I knew that was the only chance I had. Then Tim Richmond came up on him, and they got together.

"I knew then I had a good shot at it. The rains came, and I was praying for that. I just kept on digging."

He led the last five laps—the only laps he led all day.

Elliott had broken through. And he didn't sit still. Over the next nine years, he won at least one time per season, becoming one of the sport's most dominant drivers and paving the way to the NASCAR Hall of Fame.

In 1985, Elliott had a season for the ages. His Melling Racing Ford Thunderbirds had no match on NASCAR's superspeedways. He won eleven times—all on big tracks, including both races at Atlanta, Darlington, Pocono, and Michigan. Practically the only significant thing he didn't win was the series championship. Darrell Waltrip won only three races but had eighteen top fives and twenty-one top tens and took the title by 101 points over Elliott, despite the fact that Elliott led 1,920 laps to Waltrip's 969.

A very big prize did go Elliott's way that season, however, and its pursuit became one of the year's biggest stories.

Series sponsor R. J. Reynolds Tobacco Co. posted a million-dollar bonus for any driver who could win at least three of what then were known as the Big Four races—the Daytona 500, the Winston 500 at Talladega, the Coca-Cola 600 at Charlotte, and the Southern 500 at Darlington.

Bill Elliott holds a NASCAR record that is likely to stand forever. In May 1987 he led qualifying at Talladega Superspeedway with a lap of 212.809 miles per hour, easily a record. Speeds at the tour's biggest tracks have been choked by engine restrictor plates since that weekend, meaning Elliott's speed probably will never be topped.

Bill Elliott started his career in family-owned race cars but later drove for some of the sport's leading team owners. *Dick Conway*

Elliott rolled into the late-summer heat of Darlington Raceway that season with two Big Four wins and the $1 million on the line. Much of the motorsports world was focused on one of racing's oldest tracks that weekend, and Elliott's team arrived loaded for bear. South Carolina Highway Patrol troopers kept the curious from his team's garage stall throughout the race weekend so there would be no interruptions in work.

The plan couldn't have worked better. Elliott led one hundred laps and finished 0.6 of a second in front of Cale Yarborough. As Elliott drove into victory lane, fake dollar bills carrying an image of his face rained down on the team. It was one of the biggest moments of the decade for NASCAR.

"The car wasn't as quick as it could have been, but, at the end of the day, we survived, and the rest of the guys didn't," Elliott said. "Things just kind of unfolded and fell into my favor, but it was just one of them days that luck was on your side."

The success of that season—and much of that recorded during his career—saw Elliott's brothers working alongside him. Ernie Elliott built the team's engines and worked race days as crew chief; Dan Elliott worked on engines and gears and changed tires during races.

In 1988, Elliott won the series championship in a relative breeze, scoring six wins and leading the points for the final ten races. He would move on to drive for team owners Junior Johnson and Ray Evernham.

A run that began in a small shop in Dawsonville, Georgia, had taken Elliott to the top of his sport—one of the fastest men alive on a journey from rags to riches.

Elliott's career received a boost in 1981 when Michigan businessman Harry Melling bought the family team from Bill's father, George Elliott. Bill Elliott remained on board as the team driver, and Melling's financial input lifted the team to another level.

CHAPTER 28

Benny Parsons

South Boston (VA) Speedway, May 9, 1971

I t was Mother's Day, May 9, 1971, and the phone rang in a house in North Wilkesboro, North Carolina.

This was no normal Mother's Day phone call. Benny Parsons, in his second full season in NASCAR Cup Series racing, was calling from Virginia with good news. He had scored his first race win.

The phone was handed to Parsons's five-year-old son, Kevin, who listened to his father describe the win. Kevin's first question: "Was Richard Petty there?"

This was no idle question. In 1970, Petty won eighteen times. In 1971, he would win twenty-one races. In short, he was expected to win every time he took a green flag. So Kevin Parsons could be forgiven for wondering if racing's king had somehow missed the race his father won.

Indeed, Petty was there. He finished second, a lap down to Parsons.

The breakthrough win for Parsons was scored in what became the final Cup race at 0.357-mile South Boston (Virginia) Speedway. The Cup schedule was shortened dramatically for the 1972 season, and South Boston was one of the short tracks that didn't survive the cut.

Parsons was twenty-nine years old when he logged that first win. It was his sixty-sixth race in the series.

After a championship career in ARCA racing, Benny Parsons moved to Cup and won a title and the Daytona 500. *Dick Conway*

Parsons had enjoyed success in the Automobile Racing Club of America, winning the series championship in 1968 and 1969 before making the next logical step into NASCAR. Kevin, the older of his two sons, stored memories of his dad's numerous ARCA wins and wasn't impressed when the NASCAR road turned out to be so rough.

"My brother had grown up going to victory lanes with Dad," said Keith Parsons, Benny's younger son. "He famously would tell Dad, 'You need to give up on NASCAR and go back to ARCA so we can win.'"

There wasn't much give-up in Benny Parsons. Although he struggled at times and often wondered if there would be enough money to make it to the next race, his perseverance prevailed. He ultimately scored twenty-one Cup victories, won the 1973 national championship, and, after retirement, enjoyed a successful second career in race broadcasting.

Parsons died of cancer in 2007. He was inducted into the NASCAR Hall of Fame in 2017.

In 1971, Parsons was driving for North Carolina businessman and track owner L. G. DeWitt, whose team was underfunded in comparison to the big guns of the day. The landmark win at South Boston was big for Parsons and the team in many ways, but it was overshadowed soon after when DeWitt was involved in a serious passenger car accident.

"They shut the team down for several weeks," Keith Parsons said. "You would think that the win would set them up for success, but the car accident was really bad, and, for a while, it was touch-and-go if they would ever come back to racing."

The team missed six races in the heart of the 1971 season, including the popular July race at Daytona International Speedway.

"It was a trying time," Keith said. "My dad talked about it some. He didn't know what he was going to do. He had built his life on trying to race. Somebody in Nashville knew he was struggling and flew him to town every Saturday to run the weekly short-track race there."

That somebody was Nashville track promoter Bill Donoho, who not only provided Parsons with a car to race but also let him stay in the Donoho home on those race weekends.

DeWitt soon recovered, and his team, with Parsons driving and managing daily operations, returned to the Cup series in late July at Nashville. Parsons finished third. The race winner? Richard Petty, of course.

"I think winning that first race at South Boston was big for him," Keith said. "Richard Petty was always my dad's hero. I guess he was everybody's hero. He was the person everybody was trying to beat.

"Dad believed he could do it and was very results-driven. He hadn't won in a year and a half, and he came from ARCA, where he was the hot shoe. He expected more of himself. He felt like that first win really validated his decision to uproot his

Throughout his career, Parsons was often identified as "a former taxi driver from Detroit." It's true that he worked in his father's service station–taxi business, but it was largely as a manager and mechanic. He drove taxis only occasionally, usually when a regular driver missed work.

family from Detroit and move to a tiny town in Richmond County in North Carolina."

Parsons was born in North Carolina, but his father moved the family to Detroit when Benny was two. Although Benny spent most of his childhood in North Carolina with his great-grandmother, he moved to Detroit after high school to work with his father in the elder Parsons's service station and taxi business. He soon volunteered to work with a local short-track team, and his long road to racing success had begun.

Parsons won the Cup championship in 1973 in one of racing's unusual finishes. Parsons had a significant point lead entering the final race at North Carolina Motor Speedway and needed only to finish about half the laps to secure the title. But he was involved in an accident only thirteen laps into the race, and his car was heavily damaged. His shot at the championship was hanging by a thread, but members of other crews joined Parsons and his crew and repaired the damage in about an hour. Parsons returned to the track and finished enough laps to secure the title.

For years, Parsons hosted a Christmas party for underprivileged children in his hometown of Ellerbe, North Carolina. Santa made an appearance, and there were presents for all. Parsons often talked of a small boy who walked up to him at the party after receiving new sneakers and asked if he really could keep them.

In 1975, Parsons scored his biggest win, taking the checkered in the Daytona 500 after leader David Pearson spun out with six miles to go. As a sign of the respect Parsons had earned in NASCAR, members of opposing crews stood to applaud him as he drove to victory lane.

"Here's what I can say about Benny Parsons," said Tex Powell, a mechanic who worked with Parsons. "You could walk into any garage area and ask anyone who their five favorite people were, and Benny would be on all of those lists."

CHAPTER 29

Michael McDowell

Daytona (FL) International Speedway, Feb. 14, 2021

Mention the name Michael McDowell to most race fans, and their first memory is his epic qualifying wreck at Texas Motor Speedway in 2008. Only later will someone add, "Oh, yeah . . . and isn't he the guy who won the 2021 Daytona 500?"

Indeed, for much of his career the defining moment on McDowell's resume was the horrific Texas crash. But mercifully, everything changed after he led only the last lap to win the 2021 Daytona 500 in one of the biggest upsets in its sixty-three-year history.

"I don't take myself too seriously, so I'm okay with people knowing me best for that wreck in Texas," McDowell said. "It's been about fourteen years, and people still ask me about it. It's not going away, but I'm glad there's something else to talk about, something like the Daytona 500."

First, the crash that's been on every wreck-themed TV show for years:

It was April 4, 2008, and McDowell was on his two-lap qualifying run for the Samsung 500. Texas was his second Cup start—he was twenty-sixth the previous weekend at Martinsville—but his first in the Car of Tomorrow on a big track. He was approaching Turn One moments after workers had spread Speedy-dry to clean up after David Gilliland's blown motor.

"I got into the Speedy-dry and went high in Turn One," he recalled. "The car took a hard right, went almost head-on into the wall, then started barrel-rolling thirteen times. [Other views show eight to ten.] I was holding on, riding it out because there was nothing I could do."

FOX TV commentator Darrell Waltrip could barely contain himself. "Oh, no," he yelled as McDowell's car dipped left, then snapped around and went up the banking, into the SAFER barrier. His No. 34 Ford ricocheted off the wall and bounced on its roof several times before starting to twist and roll and tumble down the track. "Oh, my gosh. I have never seen anything like that," Waltrip continued. "He hit the wall a ton. It's incredible how hard he hit."

Start to finish, the accident took fourteen seconds and covered a quarter-mile from the top of Turn One to the apron in Turn Two. What remained of the car settled on all fours as a small fire erupted under the hood. After a moment to compose himself, McDowell climbed out, chatted with safety workers, surveyed the damage, and walked to the waiting ambulance, no worse for wear.

"I wiggled my toes after it stopped and realized I wasn't hurt," he said. "As I was climbing out the biggest thing on my mind was, 'Oh, man, I hope I don't get fired for this.' You know, being a rookie in only his second Cup start and then wrecking. I didn't realize how bad it was until I was in the [infield] care center and it was on television. That's when I thought, 'Man, that was bad . . . but it could have been worse.' I guess I was pretty lucky."

McDowell reached Cup after years of road racing success. He raced mostly in sports cars and open-wheel before getting to stock cars in 2006. He ran partial ARCA, Camping World, Xfinity, and Cup schedules for several owners between 2008 and 2017. In 2018, when his career

McDowell was the fortieth different Daytona 500 winner and its eighth first-race winner in its sixty-four years. The others: Tiny Lund, Mario Andretti, Pete Hamilton, Derrike Cope, Sterling Marlin, Michael Waltrip, and Trevor Bayne.

The 2021 Daytona 500 was the third victory for Front Row Motorsports and owner Bob Jenkins: David Ragan at Talladega in May of 2013, Chris Buescher at Pocono in August of 2016, and Michael McDowell at Daytona Beach in February of 2021.

might have stalled, he began his full-schedule relationship with Ford-based Front Row Motorsports.

He's mature enough to know that anything worth having is worth working for. "I've never thought much about people's perception of me because I know how hard I worked to get here," he said. "It's hard to make it in this sport and hard to stay when you finally get here. So, when people talk about the wreck, that's fine with me."

Next, the 2021 Daytona 500 and its typical last-lap drama:

McDowell was zero for 358 in Cup when he started his tenth "Great American Race" on February 14, 2021. (It ended after midnight following a six-hour rain interruption.) For most of the first 499 miles, it seemed he was headed for zero for 359. He was running fourth in the waning laps, but the front trio of Joey Logano, Kevin Harvick, and Brad Keselowski showed no signs of weakening.

He moved to third on the next-to-last lap, tagging along as Keselowski took second from Harvick approaching Turn Three. Seconds later, McDowell pushed Keselowski to within inches of Logano. As Keselowski began a low-side pass nearing Turn Three, Logano came down to block. They came together when Keselowski's right-front bumper met Logano's left rear.

When they lost control—Logano slid low, Keselowski went high—a huge hole opened for the new leader. Chase Elliott and Austin Dillon followed McDowell through the opening and were bunched together when the caution lights began flashing. Scorers needed almost a minute to ensure that McDowell was leading when he crossed the first scoring line past the accident scene. The official margin of victory was "under caution," but in reality the margin of victory was less than a car-length.

McDowell started the 500 as a 100-to-1 underdog, but didn't need Las Vegas bookies to tell him that. He'd finished top five only three times in his 358 previous starts and was top ten only twelve times. Popular with almost everyone around the sport and a man of deep and abiding faith, he knew he was lucky.

"I just can't believe it," he said afterward. "I've got to thank God. So many years [fourteen seasons] just grinding it out and hoping for an opportunity like this. We had our Ford partners [Logano and Keselowski] at the end and they crashed. Luckily, I was able to make it through. I'm so thankful.

"I had a plan that coming to five left, I'd stick to Brad's bumper," McDowell told interviewers. "I knew he was going to take a shot, and I figured if I stayed right on his bumper coming off Four [on the last lap] I'd make my move. Then Brad and Joey got together, the seas parted, and I went through the middle. It went just how we needed it to go."

CHAPTER 30

Tony Stewart

Richmond (VA) Raceway, Sept. 11, 1999

I t's been generally accepted for decades that A. J. Foyt and Mario Andretti are America's most accomplished racers. Foyt, from Texas, and Andretti, from Pennsylvania by way of Italy, have done just about everything you could ask of a driver.

When it comes to across-the-board excellence, only one American comes close to those two legends on racing's "Mini-Rushmore": Indiana–born and reared Tony Stewart.

When "Smoke" retired from NASCAR after the 2016 season, he had forty-nine Cup Series victories, eleven in the Xfinity Series, and two in the Camping World Truck Series. He had three Cup Series championship trophies and one from the Indy Racing League. Before going stock car racing, he was a USAC Triple Crown champion, a USAC Midget champion, and an IROC champion. As an open-wheel team owner, he has twenty-one championships from seven drivers. And he partners with Gene Haas in Stewart-Haas Racing, a two-time Cup championship–winning company featuring Kevin Harvick, Aric Almirola, Chase Briscoe, and Cole Custer.

Surely, all that gets him on the mythical podium with Foyt and Andretti.

Tony Stewart
left IndyCar
racing to
pursue success
in NASCAR
and won for
the first time
at Richmond
Raceway.
NIGEL KINRADE

Consider just part of their resumes:

Foyt won four Indy 500s and endurance races at LeMans, Sebring, and Daytona Beach. He won seven IndyCar national championships, a record sixty-seven IndyCar races, seven NASCAR Cup Series races (including a Daytona 500), and countless open-wheel dirt-track races.

Andretti won an Indy 500, a Formula 1 World Driving Championship, twelve F-1 races, a Daytona 500, a record sixty-seven IndyCar poles, fifty-two IndyCar victories, four IndyCar national championships, an IROC title, and a LeMans class victory. He and Foyt shared the AP's award as co–Drivers of the Twentieth Century.

Pretty heady stuff.

Even if much of Stewart's fame and success came during twenty-two years in NASCAR, he started winning go-kart and quarter-midget races as an Indiana preteen. He advanced through USAC midgets, sprint cars, and Silver Crown in the early 1990s and quickly became a popular star in the fledgling (and short-lived) Indy Racing League.

His career path swerved dramatically in 1996. With IndyCar racing in disarray, he ran nine Xfinity races for former Cup Series team-owner Harry Ranier. Drawn to Stewart's potential, Ranier and his son, Lorin, recruited him to showcase their return to NASCAR after a short break.

Over the next three seasons Stewart drove thirty-six Xfinity races (without much notable success) for the Raniers, Bobby Labonte, and Joe Gibbs. In 1999, the Raniers "sold" him to Gibbs, who built a Cup entry around him. With that first Joe Gibbs Racing contract, Stewart's lifestyle turned from Indiana-based open-wheel to Southern-based NASCAR.

Predictably, he was a quick study. His first Cup top ten was a sixth at Darlington, the fifth start of his rookie season. His first top five was four races later, a fifth at Talladega. Over the next fifteen races, his dozen top-ten finishes brought him near the top in points en route to a final fourth-place ranking. In the No. 20 Home Depot Pontiac, Stewart was the landslide Rookie of the Year winner over Elliott Sadler.

The first of his forty-nine Cup victories came in just his twenty-fifth start, among the quickest by a rookie in recent history. It came in September of 1999 at the three-quarter-mile Richmond Raceway with Greg Zipadelli coaching from the pit box. It's understandable that Stewart, now fifty-two, rolls his eyes and shakes his head when asked what he remembers about that sold-out Saturday night in Richmond.

In 2001, Stewart became the second driver (after John Andretti in 1994) to start and finish both the Indy 500 and the Coca-Cola 600 on the same day. He was sixth in the 500 and third in the 600, the first driver to complete all six hundred laps and the 1,100 miles.

Tony Stewart won Cup championships in 2002, 2005, and 2011.
DAVID GRIFFIN

"Mostly, I remember we led three hundred thirty-three of four hundred laps," he said. "But I also remember falling back to eighth or something every time we pitted. I had to be patient every time and work my way back to the front. When we got there, the caution came out again, and we pitted and fell back again. It seemed like every time we got toward the front, the caution came out and we lost positions in the pits."

It became so bad that after one series of stops the late ESPN announcer Bob Jenkins pointed out, "Stewart's getting killed on pit stops." If not for those stumbles, he may well have led all but the first few laps. As it was, the race was primarily a four-car show among Stewart, Labonte, Jeff Gordon, and Jeff Burton. (Mark Martin and pole-winner Mike Skinner led briefly but weren't serious threats.)

"We had the best car that night and probably passed more guys than anybody," Stewart recalled. "No question, that was a night when everything went right except in the pits. And all those guys we passed coming back toward the front? Jeff Gordon. Dale Jarrett. Bobby Labonte. Rusty Wallace. Dale Earnhardt. Mark Martin. Pretty good racers, all of them. It was tough passing them the first time, but they didn't have anything for us later on. We just went right on by them."

Skinner, Stewart, and Gordon swapped the lead seven times in the first half, with Stewart (all but twenty-four laps) clearly in charge. His pit stops at 56 and 105 maintained his lead, but he lost two positions at 171, three more at 214, and three more at 242. "We had a rookie driver, a rookie team, and a rookie pit crew," Stewart said of the bad stops. "But still . . ." He stopped there and slowly shook his head at the wonder of it all.

He wasn't seriously challenged beyond halfway, even coming forward from laps 214–256 after yet another slow stop. He went ahead for good at 257, shortly before Gordon and Martin began to fade. His last stop, at 304, kept him comfortably ahead to the finish. He finished more than a full second ahead of Labonte.

Later in the fall, Stewart won back-to-back at Phoenix and Homestead, setting a record for rookie victories. "That was after I'd figured it out and Zippy had figured it out, and we had figured it out together," he said of those late-season victories. "I don't think anybody sits down and thinks about when they're going to win one of these things. You just try your best every time you go out there. That's what we did that night in Richmond."

> Stewart won at least one Cup race a year for fifteen consecutive years, from his rookie season of 1999 through 2013. He was winless in 2014–2015, then got the last of his forty-nine victories in 2016.

CHAPTER 31

Ned Jarrett

Myrtle Beach (SC) Speedway, Aug. 1, 1959

The celebration of Ned Jarrett's first NASCAR Cup Series victory was somewhat abbreviated for a very good reason. Jarrett's right hand had been cut to the bone during the race and was bleeding profusely.

This is not the sort of first-win "victory lane" most drivers have in their dreams.

It was part of a crazy weekend in 1959 for Jarrett, who had won NASCAR's Late Model Sportsman national championship in 1957 and 1958 and was looking to stake his claim in stock car racing's top series with a victory. To make that jump, Jarrett realized he needed a top-flight car. "I knew I could do it if I could get in the right car," he said.

The "right car" became available in the summer of 1959. Junior Johnson had scored a series of Cup wins in a 1957 Ford for car owner Paul Spaulding. Spaulding worked out a deal to build a new Dodge for Johnson, making the Ford suddenly available. But there was a problem. The sale price was $2,000.

"Dad didn't have $20, much less $2,000," said Glenn Jarrett, Ned's son.

What Jarrett did have was confidence—overflowing, semi-dangerous confidence. With back-to-back races coming up on the first two days

139

of August at Myrtle Beach (South Carolina) Speedway and Charlotte (North Carolina) Fairgrounds Speedway, he saw his opportunity. Jarrett bought the car on Saturday with a $2,000 check with the knowledge that the check wouldn't hit his account until Monday.

"I didn't have any money," Jarrett said. "I figured I'd go to Myrtle Beach Saturday night and win that race and do the same thing the next afternoon at Charlotte. I knew winning both would earn about $2,000, and I could make up whatever difference there was by borrowing the money and get in to the bank by Monday to cover the check."

And that's exactly what happened. Jarrett won Saturday night at Myrtle Beach, finishing a lap ahead of Jim Paschal for his first Cup victory. He and crew chief Bud Allman worked overnight to refine the car for Sunday's race at Charlotte. Jarrett, with relief driving from Junior Johnson and Joe Weatherly, won that race, with Paschal again finishing second.

Jarrett owns the NASCAR record for largest margin of victory. He won the 1965 Southern 500 at Darlington Raceway by fourteen laps. Buck Baker was a woeful second.

Jarrett's weekend winnings totaled about $1,800, and he was able to quickly borrow the rest to cover the check. It was a gamble that worked marvelously, a kind of business plan that unfolded perfectly. But the story is about much more than Jarrett's bold tight-rope walk with a potential bounced check.

It's also about blood, and likely sweat and tears. But especially blood.

Because Jarrett bought his new car on race-day Saturday and he and Allman, a widely respected mechanic of the day, had to rush to coastal South Carolina for the night race, there wasn't time to cover all the bases in preparing the car. Among the areas that weren't addressed was the steering wheel, which was stock equipment in those days. To make gripping the hard wheel over bumpy dirt tracks more comfortable, it was typical to put a ring of foam rubber around the wheel and then wrap it with electrical tape.

"Whoever had put the tape on wrapped it the wrong way," Jarrett said. "When they cut it, it left edges of the tape sticking up, and it cut into my hand [he didn't wear gloves] every time I turned the car. The track was rough, and I could feel it cutting the meat to the bone, and I could feel the blood coming out. But I had a job to do."

Jarrett had raced Myrtle Beach in Sportsman cars, so he had a course of attack. "The track always got rough when they put those heavy cars on it," he said. "I had to dodge the holes that would come in the track. I worked for a while to get a groove built. I ran higher than the other drivers. They were in the regular groove. I worked to build a groove higher on the track. It took about a hundred laps, and I got lapped while I was doing it, but when it got worked out I set sail, unlapped myself, and then lapped the field."

Jarrett concentrated so much on building his own groove—"an inch at a time," as he put it—that he didn't realize the extent to which his hands were being damaged. "I could sort of feel it," he said, "but I didn't realize they were as bad as they were."

Jarrett toughed it out through two hundred laps and took the first checkered flag of his Cup career. He stopped the car at the start-finish line for the trophy ceremony, which couldn't proceed until someone wrapped a tourniquet around his hand to slow the blood flow.

"It wasn't your typical victory lane," Jarrett understated.

Jarrett and Allman left the track with their winning car and Jarrett's first Cup trophy. Jarrett's hand was still throbbing with pain and was bleeding. They stopped at a hospital in nearby Conway.

Common sense called for Jarrett to take time off for his wounds to heal. The emergency room doctor also called for that. But Jarrett had a check to cover.

"At the hospital, they wrapped it up and put antiseptic of some kind on it," Jarrett said. "The doctor said I needed to let it heal, that I couldn't drive for at least two weeks. I told him what the situation was and what I had to do and that I had to race—and win—on Sunday in Charlotte. He didn't think that was too smart."

They drove on to Jarrett's Charlotte shop and worked on the car much of the night before heading to the fairgrounds track for the afternoon race.

Jarrett declared himself ready to race, but just barely. "I was a total physical wreck," he said. "But I was able to start the race even though I was still hurting."

Jarrett lasted about half of the race over the rough half-mile dirt track. He realized he couldn't finish the race, so he pitted and turned the car over to driver Joe Weatherly, who was at the track but wasn't competing. Weatherly drove the car for a while before Junior Johnson, whose car blew an engine, climbed in to finish the race in first place. Because he had won in the Ford repeatedly before it was sold to Jarrett, he was very familiar with the car and its particular strengths.

As the driver who started the race in the winning car, Jarrett got credit for the victory—and the first-place check.

"Neither Joe nor Junior would take any money for driving," Jarrett said. "They knew I needed it. Word had gotten around that I had given a bad check."

Before the weekend, Jarrett was broke and had no Cup wins. After the weekend, he had two Cup victories and was off to the races.

Jarrett's back was broken in a crash at Greenville-Pickens Speedway in South Carolina in 1965, his second championship season. Jarrett didn't miss a race, but the injury was a health issue for the veteran driver for many years.

"I think it opened some doors, and I proved to myself that I could do it," Jarrett said. "I was cocky enough to believe that I could do it. The car had proven that it could win races. It was a big step for me in getting in the right car at the right time."

Jarrett went on to win the Cup championship in 1961 and 1965, scoring fifty race victories along the way. He retired in 1966 and later had a successful career in race broadcasting. He was elected to the NASCAR Hall of Fame as a member of the 2011 class.

The trophy Jarrett won on that remarkable night in Myrtle Beach remains on display in the recreation room at his North Carolina home, alongside other sports trophies won by his sons Dale and Glenn.

CHAPTER 32

Kyle Busch

Auto Club (CA) Speedway, Sept. 4, 2005

Kyle Busch doesn't mean to sound boastful—no, really, he doesn't—when he says there are simply too many NASCAR victories for him to rank them in importance. Going into the 2022 season, the younger of the Busch brothers has won 222 times in NASCAR's top three classes: 59 in the Cup Series, a record 102 in the Xfinity Series, and a record 61 in the Camping World Truck Series.

Each has been special in its own way . . . unique and unforgettable for all time. Late-life reflection might help establish a pecking order in time, but not yet.

Without much debate, he considers the 2005 SONY HD 500 the highlight of his Cup career. "The first ones in each series are special because they were the first ones," Busch said. "Fontana in 2005 was extra sweet because of what had happened there before. It was special, but it's hard to give it a ranking because there have been so many."

Asking Busch to rank them all is like asking Tom Brady to rank his seven Super Bowl victories or asking a new mother which of the newborn twins is her favorite. They're all tied for first.

In November of 2001, as a sixteen-year-old Las Vegas short-track hot-shot, Busch was barred from Fontana's one-hundred-lap, two-hundred-

Kyle Busch followed his older brother, Kurt, into NASCAR and quickly became one of the tour's hottest drivers. *David Griffin*

mile Camping World race. Team owner Jack Roush pulled him because he was too young at the time (eighteen was the minimum) for a "big-track" race. With his Truck team already on hand, Roush replaced Busch in the No. 99 Ford with California native Tim Woods.

Three years later, in September of 2004, Busch was back at Fontana, this time old enough to drive the No. 84 Chevrolet for Hendrick Motorsports. In his third career Cup start, the eighteen-year-old started eighteenth and finished a lap down in twenty-fourth. In February of 2005, fully entrenched as a Cup regular, Busch won the pole and finished a lap down twenty-third. It was a tiny improvement over his previous Fontana runs, but nevertheless a sign of things to come.

Later that same 2005 season, in September, Busch finally broke through at Fontana. In his thirty-first career start, he qualified twenty-fifth, led 95 of 254 laps (the race went overtime) for the first of his fifty-nine (and counting) Cup victories. Ten starts and less than three months later, he led sixty-three laps to win at Phoenix and easily lock up Rookie of the Year.

"There was a lot of redemption with that first win at Fontana," said Busch, a four-time winner there. "You know, from not being allowed to run the Truck race because I was too young to coming back and winning in just my third time there. As it's turned out, I've had pretty good success there. I enjoy going out to California."

"Pretty good" is an understatement. Busch has eleven top-five finishes, seventeen top tens, and only one DNF in his twenty-two Fontana starts. He's completed 99 percent of the available laps en route to an average finish of 9.6. (In addition to that first Chevy victory with Hendrick, he has three victories in Toyotas for Joe Gibbs Racing.) He's been top ten in nine of his last ten starts there (including three victories) and had nine consecutive top-ten finishes during another ten-race stretch early in his career.

He surprised himself with that first Cup victory on Labor Day weekend of 2005. His No. 5 Carquest Chevrolet was nothing special in the early stages, but got better as the warm afternoon moved into a slightly cooler night. He had a comfortable lead and was virtually home free until a debris caution in the final laps let the field catch up.

After calling for four tires under the last caution, crew chief Alan Gustafson calmly switched to rights-only because

Kyle (2015 and 2019) and Kurt (2004) Busch are among two sets of brothers to win Cup Series championships, along with Terry (1984 and 1998) and Bobby (2000) Labonte. Kyle (2009) and Bobby (1991) also won Xfinity Series championships.

Busch had stopped too close to the wall for a left-side change. He restarted third with fourteen laps remaining, and despite the two-tire handicap, easily passed Jeff Green and Robby Gordon and took the lead for good.

"I didn't think we had a winning car at first," Busch recalled. "But it suddenly got better about halfway through the race. It was outrunning some of the guys who were the superstars of the series at the time. I was ahead of [spring race winner] Greg Biffle and Matt Kenseth, two of Roush's guys back when that was a powerhouse team."

Kyle Busch and the M&M's-sponsored car became familiar sights in
victory lane. *David Griffin*

When a late caution bunched the field again and forced overtime,
Busch never flinched. "I started feeling good with five laps to go, when
the guys weren't catching me [before the last caution]," he said. "But I
didn't know I had it won until I came off Turn Four on the last overtime lap and nobody was there." (Biffle was close, but not nearly close
enough; the margin of victory was a half-second.) "It was really cool to
be able to do my first burnout and celebrate with all the flashbulbs and
lights and the speedway's fireworks," Busch said.

At twenty years, four months, and two days, Busch became NASCAR's
youngest Cup winner. At nineteen years, one month, and four days, Joey
Logano took the record by winning a rain-shortened race at Loudon,

Jimmie Johnson (2002) and Kyle Busch (2005) are the only Cup Series drivers to record their first career victory at California (Auto Club) Speedway. All told, eighteen different drivers have been to victory lane in the thirty-one races since the track opened in 1997.

New Hampshire, in June of 2009. At twenty years and one day, Trevor Bayne became NASCAR's second-youngest winner at the 2011 Daytona 500.

There were years when Busch ran two or three races almost every weekend—sometimes at different venues—and generally won at least one of them. His 222 victories might have been closer to 250 if NASCAR hadn't limited full-time, experienced Cup drivers to a few lower-series races each season. He once admitted wanting to win 300 races over the three series, a goal that now seems unattainable.

No surprise here: he's not happy about the rule limiting Cup drivers to five Xfinity and five Truck races a year. Busch says it's important for him to run more races to help fund Kyle Busch Motorsports as it fields cars and trucks for young drivers hoping to move up. Also, no surprise here: NASCAR seems disinclined to soften that rule.

CHAPTER 33

Chase Elliott

Watkins Glen (NY) International, Aug. 5, 2018

C hase Elliott could count the close calls as they stacked up in the early years of his NASCAR Cup Series career.

And, if he wasn't counting, other people were.

In 2016, his first full season at stock car racing's top level, he had two second-place finishes and ten top fives with no victories. The following season he boosted both numbers—five seconds and a dozen top fives, but, again, no wins.

The 2018 season dawned with the full expectation that it would be the year that Elliott and his top-flight Hendrick Motorsports team jumped the last hurdle. It took twenty-two races—and yet another close-call second place—but Elliott scored August 5 at Watkins Glen International in New York.

When the win finally arrived, it almost seemed easy (if Cup wins are ever easy). Elliott led fifty-two laps, including the final thirty-four, and finished a startling seven seconds in front of second-place Martin Truex Jr. In a series in which road-course races often have turned into every-man-for-himself, last-lap calamities, Elliott was on cruise control.

In Dawsonville, Georgia, the siren at the Dawsonville Pool Room—the loud and lasting herald of an Elliott family victory—sounded, and

After a string of second-place finishes, Chase Elliott crossed over into victory lane in 2018 at Watkins Glen International. Here he pits at Las Vegas Motor Speedway. *DAVID GRIFFIN*

the success envisioned by many for Chase Elliott turned from promise to reality. (Chase once worked at the Pool Room as a dishwasher.)

Two more wins followed that season, and Elliott won five times in 2020 on the way to his first Cup championship. For a driver from whom much was expected, the future had arrived.

Chase Elliott's name is actually William Clyde Elliott II. He was named for his father, Bill, who rarely is called either William or Clyde. So why Chase? Mary Colwell, a friend of Bill and Cindy Elliott (Chase's mother), was at the hospital when he was born. "She was holding him and looked down at him and said, 'Well, I'm sorry, he doesn't look like a William to me. I think I'll call him Chase,'" Cindy said. And "Chase" it continues to be, from firesuits to autographs.

"We needed to get to victory lane," Elliott said. "The thing that kept me going and kept me driven was that every time we did our best at practice and qualifying and executing the race, we had a shot to win. It was just about extracting that more often.

"That's always a challenge, but I had had enough close calls to where I thought we had everything to be successful. We just had to put it together and be solid. It was a good day to check the box."

Elliott has become one of racing's best road-course drivers, but before the big splash at Watkins Glen he admitted that the oh-so-close finishes across the landscape of the Cup tour were beginning to wear on him.

"Certainly, there were enough close calls before that race to hurt your confidence a little bit," he said. "But I felt like we were good up there that weekend, although I didn't feel like we were as good as it turned out. Sometimes you don't really know where you stand until the race starts. It takes a while to figure it out."

As the son of former Cup champion Bill Elliott, Chase arrived in the sport carrying big expectations. He raced his first full season in the second-level Xfinity Series in 2014 and almost immediately announced his intentions to stir the pot. In the April race at tough old Darlington Raceway, Elliott, eighteen, charged to the front on the final lap after passing five cars, and won, leaving much more experienced drivers Matt Kenseth, Kyle Busch, Joey Logano, and Kevin Harvick in his wake.

That dramatic win was a wakeup call for anyone who thought Elliott might have been rushed into the Xfinity Series too early. He also had won the previous race at Texas Motor Speedway, but to score on the last lap at treacherous Darlington, a track whose characteristics don't lend themselves

Chase and Bill, son and father, raced against each other in 2013 in a Late Model race on an Alabama short track. Chase won the race; his dad finished fourth. "I followed him around for a while," Bill said. "When he decided to go, he was gone. I never saw him again."

to last-lap heroics, lifted the drama to another level. It was the kind of win that drew broad attention in the NASCAR garage area, and it impressed even his father, who scored forty-four Cup wins, including five at Darlington.

"I look at him winning at Texas, and that was unbelievable," Bill said. "But then you look at Darlington, and I was just amazed, shaking my head, at how he went about it. You go out sixth with two laps to go at Darlington, and you don't have a very good chance to win the race. And he did it. You have to keep in mind that he had never been to Texas, never been to Darlington, never run a lap at those places."

CHAPTER 34

Geoff Bodine

Martinsville (VA) Speedway, Apr. 29, 1984

I t's perhaps surprising to learn how close Hendrick Motorsports (HMS) came to shutting down three months into the 1984 NASCAR Cup Series season. The Charlotte-based company might have gone under if crew chief Harry Hyde and driver Geoff Bodine hadn't delivered its first victory to rookie owner Rick Hendrick.

It was April of 1984, and Hendrick had decided to quit stock car racing after just a handful of starts. He was disappointed with his team's performance and shocked by how quickly he was spending his money. He knew racing was costly, but never expected to blow most of his budget by springtime.

"I thought there was nothing to do but shut down," Hendrick said of those bleak days in 1984. "I didn't know how much longer we could go on. I was just getting started in the automobile business and running the team out of my pocket. I couldn't afford to lose money at the rate we were losing. In the open weekend after Darlington, I was ready to shut down."

But the next race was at Martinsville Speedway in southern Virginia, where Hendrick was born and reared. When he told Hyde the team might skip that race, the crusty ol' crew chief pushed back. "Harry kept

Geoff Bodine gave team owner Rick Hendrick his first Cup victory in 1984. *DAVID GRIFFIN*

saying, 'Just let us go to Martinsville,'" Hendrick remembered. "He said, 'Bodine is good there; we can win.' Well, he talked me into it, and off they go. We won the race and got a sponsor out of it, and the rest is history because Harry talked me into it."

Ironically, Hendrick and his wife, Linda, were at a church retreat that Sunday and missed seeing the No. 5 Chevrolet give them their first victory. Bodine, in his sixty-ninth career Cup start and eighth for HMS, started sixth on the flat, demanding half-mile oval. He drove well and stayed close all day, clearly the startup team's best effort. He led laps 215–220 and again from 452 to 500, winning by six seconds over Ron Bouchard.

Hendrick recalled the buildup to that day, one that changed both his life and Bodine's and began setting a standard for motorsports excellence unsurpassed in this country.

"I went to that year's Daytona 500 and stood on the grid with owners like Richard Petty, Junior Johnson, and Richard Childress," he said years later. "I looked around and thought, 'What am I doing here?' I honestly hoped to someday win even one race. We had five full-time

employees and 5,000 square feet of leased
space, and I was running the team out of my
own pocket. I could afford to do that for only
so long if we didn't find a sponsor."

Hendrick couldn't pick up the Martinsville
broadcast, so he checked with his mother during
a break at church. "There were no cell phones
back then," he reminded. "I called her from a
pay phone and asked about the race. She said,
dead seriously, 'You haven't heard? He blew up.'
I thought it was all over. Then she said, 'No,
he won!' I couldn't believe it. I about dropped
the phone. Then we went straight to Bodine's
house [near Greensboro] and covered his yard
in toilet paper. It was such a relief. If we hadn't
won, there's no way we'd be here today."

Bodine got the HMS ride by years of
dominance in NASCAR's lower-level Modified
Series. He was a constant threat at that level,
so much so that the 1978 Guinness Book of
Records credited him with a record fifty-five
Modified victories in eighty-four starts.

Those years of lower-level success led to
sixty-one Cup starts with several mid-pack
teams in 1979–1983. Bodine ran most of 1982

Bodine's 575-start stat line between 1979 and 2011: eighteen victories, 100 top fives, and 190 top tens. Among the victories were a Daytona 500, three road races, eight on short tracks, and six on longer speedways.

(winning Rookie of the Year) and 1983 with owner Cliff Stewart, then
joined Hendrick, who thought NASCAR would help promote his
Chevrolet dealerships.

"I guess you could say it was quite a gamble," Bodine said of his
move from Stewart to Hendrick. "I could have stayed with Cliff more
than just two seasons because we'd done okay. We had some good runs
[three poles, nine top fives, and nineteen top tens in fifty-two starts]
and might have won some races if things hadn't kept breaking.

"At the time, Rick's team didn't have much except for Harry, a race-
winning championship crew chief [1970 with Bobby Isaac]. I figured he
could teach me how to win and have a better chance than with Cliff.

Geoff Bodine used success in Modified racing to earn a place in the Cup series. *BARB SAUNDERS / BRH RACING ARCHIVES*

But Rick might have shut down if Harry hadn't convinced him to go to Martinsville. Harry said the car and the engine were ready, and I was pretty good there. Thank goodness Harry talked Rick into it."

Bodine practiced and qualified well that weekend. "I was confident," he said. "I had won there in Modifieds and Sportsman [seven victories], so I knew how to save brakes and keep the fenders on the car. It was important to save your stuff. Bobby Allison led almost all day, but he wore his stuff out. I had a better-handling car at the end, and I drove around him on the outside of Turn Four [at lap 452] and led the rest of the way."

Bodine and Hyde won twice more that year. First, they crushed Darrell Waltrip and Dale Earnhardt in a dominating midsummer rout

Bodine, now seventy-two and living in Florida, was the driving force behind the US bobsled team's success in the 2002 and 2010 Winter Olympics. He was so angry that the US was using European-built bobsleds that he created the Bo-Dyn Bobsled Project that designed, built, and financially supported American bobsleds.

at Nashville. Later, in the season finale at Riverside, they beat Tim Richmond and newly crowned series champion Terry Labonte.

Bodine stayed with Hendrick five more years, winning four more times with crew chiefs Gary Nelson, Waddell Wilson, and Richard Broome. He spent the next four years divided between Junior Johnson and Bud Moore, then formed his own team from the remnants of the late Alan Kulwicki's estate. The last of his eighteen victories came with his own team and crew chief Paul Andrews at Watkins Glen in 1996.

Bodine spent the final twelve years of his career (no victories in 143 intermittent starts) with Cup, Xfinity, and Camping World owners who meant well but didn't have the resources to get him back to victory lane. At sixty-two and in relatively good health, he retired after a few races in 2011.

CHAPTER 35

Bobby Labonte

Charlotte (NC) Motor Speedway, May 28, 1995

I t's a small, select group right now, but one that will grow in the next few years. For now, retired former two-series NASCAR champion Bobby Labonte is the only driver with championships in NASCAR's top two series *plus* a place in its Hall of Fame (HOF).

The Texas native and North Carolina resident won the 1991 Xfinity Series title with his family-owned team. Nine years later, driving for Joe Gibbs Racing, he won the 2000 NASCAR Cup Series title. Not surprisingly, he went into the 2020 NASCAR Hall of Fame with Gibbs, Buddy Baker, Waddell Wilson, and Tony Stewart.

Labonte will stay in that unique HOF category until at least five drivers join him fairly soon: Brad Keselowski, Kyle Busch, Kevin Harvick, Martin Truex Jr., and Chase Elliott already have two championship trophies and will almost certainly make the HOF.

The younger Labonte followed brother Terry to NASCAR, arriving in 1978 from Corpus Christi, Texas. He honed his skills and learned to be a champion by racing go-karts, quarter-midgets, Baby Grands, and Late Models for years in Texas and North Carolina. That led to Xfinity racing in 1990 and to full-schedule Cup racing in 1993.

Bobby Labonte scored his first victory in 1995 in NASCAR's longest race, the Coca-Cola 600 at Charlotte.
DAVID GRIFFIN

"When I was fourteen, running quarter-midgets and go-karts, I never thought about what might be," the fifty-eight-year-old recently said. "For a few years I was just dabbling in racing. Our father [Bob] had raced a little in Texas and Terry was already into Cup, so I was around racing all the time."

His success in lower series convinced him that getting to Cup was doable. With his father as crew chief, he went full-time Xfinity racing in 1990–1992. He won only five times in ninety-three starts, but was fourth, first, and second in points by finishing top five in about one-third of his starts. When Bill Davis offered a Cup ride for 1993, Labonte jumped at it.

"I was racing against Jeff Gordon and Harry Gant and Mark Martin and Dale Jarrett on Saturday afternoon, and I wasn't getting lapped," Labonte said of those days. "I was running right with them. That helped me realize I could compete with them at the next level."

The Coca-Cola 600 at Charlotte Motor Speedway in May 1995 was Labonte's 11th start with JGR, his 74th Cup start overall. (He was zero for two with his own team in 1991 and zero for sixty-one with Davis in 1993–1994). As things turned out, his twenty-one victories, twenty-five poles, and 2000 Cup title came during his eleven years (1995–2005) with JGR.

Labonte recalled his 600 victory as "fairly straightforward, nothing out of the ordinary." His No. 18 Chevrolet had been competitive early in the season, continuing what Jarrett and crew chief Jimmy Makar had built in 1992–1994. "We had good speed week in and week out," Labonte said. "We'd been fast a lot of times, so we felt we always had a chance. We'd been so close to winning [two runner-up finishes in ten starts before Charlotte], so it wasn't a stunning surprise when it finally happened.

"I'd always had good Xfinity runs at Charlotte and with Bill's Cup cars. In those 600s you had to take care of the car, and I was good at that. We didn't do anything special, like two-tire, at any point. As afternoon became night, we adjusted the car to make it better. There was no specific moment when [snap], 'That's it; that's what won us the race.' We were set up for late, so we felt we'd probably be okay if we stayed lead-lap after one hundred laps."

Maybe so, but with forty-five of four hundred laps remaining, Labonte was second to Ken Schrader. "I was catching him each lap, catching him, catching him," he said. "I was smoking fast, but I knew catching him would be one thing and passing him would be something else. I was in Turn One, closing in, when he pulled over in Turn Two; something had broken [engine failure] on his car. Earlier that night, when Jeff Gordon went out, it opened the race up for everybody. When Schrader went out, I led the last whatever [43] laps and beat Terry by about six seconds."

Bobby's 2001 International Race of Champions title made the Labontes the second set of brothers—Terry won the 1989 championship—to win the all-star series. The Unser brothers also won IROC titles—Bobby in 1975 and Al in 1978. (Al Jr. won the series in 1986 and 1988.)

One of Bobby's most memorable victories came in the 1996 season-closing NAPA 500 at Atlanta Motor Speedway. It was extra-special for the family because that was the day fifth-finishing Terry won his second Cup Series title, this one by thirty-seven points over Gordon, a teammate at Hendrick Motorsports.

The victory made the Labontes the sixth set of brothers to win in the Cup Series to that point: the Allison and Flock brothers each had ninety-four combined victories, the Thomas brothers forty-nine, the Parsons twenty-two, the Bodines eighteen, the Labontes thirteen.

"That win meant a lot, not only because it was my first, but it was the first for some of the crew," Bobby said. "Some had won with Dale Jarrett, but it was the first for some others. The other thing is that just ten months earlier I wasn't sure what I'd be doing the next year. I'd just gotten the Gibbs ride, so it was good to win so quickly. And a lot of friends and family were in victory lane. We didn't cry together, but we enjoyed it together.

"The first win for anybody is important; it catapults you up the line. That first one teaches you how to win, how to maybe get the next one. It actually makes you hungrier for the next one and the one after that. It helps you grow as a driver and teaches you so much about the sport. It was a big deal for all of us."

Labonte won twice more that year and had at least one victory a year for nine of his eleven years (1995–2005) with Gibbs. His twenty-first and last victory came at Homestead, Florida, in November 2003 in his last start for JGR. He ran ten more seasons for several second-line teams before walking away from a handful of mid-pack runs. He retired in 2016 at age fifty-two. He'll occasionally race a Late Model or Modified for a weekend "fix," but has no plans to return full-time.

"Doing what I'm doing now [building chassis for short-track and dirt-track cars] is all the fun I need. I'm about ninety-nine-point-nine percent sure the [return to NASCAR] ship has sailed," he told NASCAR.com last summer. "And I'm OK with that."

CHAPTER 36

Mark Martin

North Carolina Motor Speedway, Oct. 22, 1989

Among the enduring debates surrounding NASCAR is the one with the unanswerable question: Who's the best Cup Series driver never to have won a championship? Not the *most successful*. Not the *winningest*. Not the most *popular*. Rather . . . the *best*.

With forty-six poles and fifty victories, Hall of Fame owner/driver the late Junior Johnson is a candidate. But he never had a top-five season (his best was sixth in 1955 and 1961) and he had only four top-ten seasons.

Current driver Denny Hamlin comes to mind. Going into the 2022 season, he had thirty-three poles and forty-six victories in sixteen seasons. He's been top five in points seven times and top ten in points thirteen times. His best points season was 2010, when he finished second to Jimmie Johnson by thirty-nine points.

Then there's retired Hall of Fame driver Mark Martin, the man generally considered the uncrowned king of racing. Consider his resume:

He was a five-time championship points runner-up, twice to Dale Earnhardt and once each to Jeff Gordon, Tony Stewart, and Jimmie Johnson. He was third in points four times and had a twelve-year run (1989–2000) of top-ten seasons with owner Jack Roush. That streak

Eight years after stepping into the Cup Series for the first time, Mark Martin got win No. 1 at Rockingham, North Carolina.
DAVID GRIFFIN

grew to sixteen top-ten seasons in twenty-four years with Roush and, much later, Rick Hendrick.

Martin closed his career with three full seasons at HMS and four partial seasons with four other owners. He retired in 2013, thirty-two years after arriving as a twenty-two-year-old Midwestern short-track star. His career-ending stat line showed forty Cup victories, forty-nine Xfinity Series victories, and seven in Camping World Trucks.

In 1998, Martin was named one of NASCAR's fifty greatest drivers. In 2015, he was selected for the Motorsports Hall of Fame of America. Two years later, he went into the National Motorsports Press Association Hall of Fame. He called his 2017 summons from the NASCAR Hall of Fame the highlight of his career. He, Richard Childress, Rick Hendrick, the late Benny Parsons, and Raymond Parks went in together.

Long-time Martin fans still bristle at the $40,000 fine
and forty-six-point penalty NASCAR imposed for a small
engine irregularity after winning the 1990 spring race
at Richmond. He won six poles and two more races that
year, but finished second to Earnhardt by twenty-six
points in the championship standings.

"I never hit the super home run and didn't win the Daytona 500,"
Martin said during induction weekend five years ago. "And I didn't win
a championship. But I put a lot of emphasis on winning. Let me tell
you: I've done more in racing than I ever expected. And I mean *EVER*
expected! I'll never look back and regret what *DIDN'T* happen. Instead,
I'll look back and remember what *DID* happen."

As always . . . pure class.

Martin was driving his motorcoach to Indianapolis in May of 2016
while HOF voters were gathering in Charlotte. He was parked and
settled in, cleaning bugs off the windshield, when his phone rang.

Car No. 6 became a signature for Mark Martin. *Dick Conway*

"It just *blew up* [with calls from informed well-wishers]," he said. "I mean, my phone had never blown up like that. It was crazy, something not really expected. It was weird, so I wouldn't have voted that way myself.

"I felt a little awkward, especially during the induction because I looked up at all the flags along the wall—my heroes, the people that built the sport. I wasn't one of those guys [so] I was almost a little bit embarrassed. The hall is the crown jewel of my career. But I don't think one trophy defines an athlete. He's defined by his actions over a period of time, by what he accomplished over years. I don't think a trophy makes the man."

His emphasis on winning developed early, as a teenager on the dirt tracks of Arkansas. He went from those primitive roots to the American Speed Association (ASA), where he won twenty-two features and

Tiny but tough, Mark Martin built a reputation as one of the NASCAR tour's smartest drivers. *DICK CONWAY*

Mark Martin's first attempt at Cup racing failed, but he returned to team up with car owner Jack Roush and finish his career with forty wins.
DICK CONWAY

four championships. Among the older, more-seasoned veterans he challenged: Bobby Allison, Alan Kulwicki, Dick Trickle, Jim Sauter, and Rusty Wallace.

He moved to Cup in 1981, after the third of his four ASA titles. He struggled for consistency, running for eight owners (including himself) over five seasons. He spent all his money and all he could borrow trying to establish himself. His personal life was a mess. He had a drinking problem and was financially ruined. He found no joy in racing, the overwhelming passion of his life. Between 1981 and 1987 his prospects for a long and successful NASCAR career seemed beyond remote. He described himself as "an emotionally broken man."

Everything changed in 1987. After watching Martin dominate the ASA, Allison suggested that Roush hire him for his new 1988 Cup team. After several conversations, the deal was done, giving Martin much-needed professional and personal stability. Their discussions addressed all the important issues in racing: personnel, team finances, chassis design, engine suppliers, testing commitments, and tire management. Never once did either man mention salary.

Typically, 1988 was frustrating. In addition to ten top-ten finishes, Martin and Roush had ten DNFs. The forty-first in the Daytona 500 was balanced by a second at Bristol several weeks later. There were more finishes in the twenties and thirties than in the top fifteen. That inconsistency largely doomed the No. 6 team to fifteenth in final points.

Things changed dramatically in 1989, capped by Martin's breakthrough victory in October at Rockingham, North Carolina. He started seventh, led five times for 101 laps and beat Rusty Wallace by just over three seconds. (A late-race, two-tire pit stop gave him the track position he needed to ride to victory.) It was his 113th career Cup start and his fifty-sixth with Roush. He also had six poles that year and fourteen top-five finishes, almost half the twenty-nine-race schedule. The team finished third in points, the first of thirteen seasons it finished that well.

His reaction to that first victory after thirteen top-three finishes just years after his career was in jeopardy: "I can't believe it," he said after the four-hour race. "I feel like my whole life is fulfilled. This is a dream come true because I've wanted it so bad for so long. I'm lucky to have the opportunity to work with Jack and [team leaders] Robin Pemberton and Steve Hmiel. Right now, I feel like I have it all. This first win makes my life complete."

Odd but true: Martin's favorite music genre is . . . rap. He's a big fan of (among others) Drake, Gucci Mane, Dr. Dre, Snoop, and 50 Cent.

CHAPTER 37

Paul Goldsmith

Langhorne (PA) Speedway, Sept. 23, 1956

S uccess racing on two wheels doesn't guarantee success on four wheels, but Paul Goldsmith crossed that bridge and never slowed down.

A nationally known star in motorcycle racing in the early 1950s, Goldsmith, with the considerable help of mechanic / crew chief / racing guru Smokey Yunick, transitioned to stock cars and became one of NASCAR's finest. He raced in the Cup Series from 1956 to 1969, scoring nine wins and forty-four top fives despite running only partial schedules. He and engineer/team owner Ray Nichels were a dynamic duo for part of that period.

Goldsmith's most notable NASCAR achievement will keep his name in stock car racing record books forever. He won the final race on the famous Daytona Beach, Florida, beach-road course, steering a Yunick-owned Pontiac to a five-car-length win in 1958. A year later, Daytona International Speedway opened a few miles from the shoreline, and the beach-road course, which combined racing on the Atlantic sand with the parallel two-lane paved highway, lost to the tide of the times.

As with several other race locations, Goldsmith used experience racing motorcycles to help navigate the difficulties of the Daytona beach-road course. He also had won on motorcycles on the course.

The same dynamic helped Goldsmith score his first Cup victory September 23, 1956, at the storied Langhorne Speedway in Pennsylvania. Known as the Track That Ate the Heroes, Langhorne was one of the most dangerous speedways in the country. At least twenty-three competitors died in accidents on the near-circular one-mile track.

A lead driver for Harley-Davidson, Goldsmith won at Langhorne in 1953, one of the highlights of a motorcycle racing career that would earn him entry into the American Motorcyclist Association Hall of Fame.

Three years later, Goldsmith returned to Langhorne in a stock car and used his mental blueprint of the track to win in NASCAR for the first time, outdistancing series veteran Lee Petty by an embarrassing seven laps. He led 182 of the 300 laps.

"It was a terrible track," said Goldsmith, echoing the opinions of many drivers who ran Langhorne. "It was mainly about the kind of surface it was. Some of it was deep, some of it was shallow. It was a lot of work, but I didn't have much trouble. I could run just about wide open around the track because I knew where to go. I knew where the bumps were and where the surface changed."

The race was a grueling affair, three hundred laps around the wicked Langhorne circle. Twenty-four of the forty-four starters failed to finish the race, and the fifth-place finisher, Herb Thomas, was a full ten laps behind. Few were surprised at the power of the track to decimate the field. Driver Cotton Owens said racing at Langhorne was like "jumping a fresh-plowed field."

The race was entertaining, however, particularly as Goldsmith and emerging star Fireball Roberts, who would win five times that season, exchanged the lead over

Goldsmith's worst racing injury occurred during his motorcycle career. In a race at a track near Cleveland, he ran his bike into a fence to avoid hitting another rider. He slid off the track banking and into race traffic. A following driver ran across his feet, breaking both.

a tense series of laps. Roberts's challenge to Goldsmith ended, however, when he parked his Ford with a broken oil line.

The Langhorne win came in Goldsmith's eighth NASCAR race and made him the first competitor to take checkered flags there in motorcycle and stock car events.

Yunick, whose Daytona Beach, Florida, garage was well known as a place of motorsports mystery and magic, had been Goldsmith's "agent" as he shifted from two wheels to four.

"I met Smokey racing motorcycles on the beach at Daytona," Goldsmith said, remembering the moment sixty-five years later. "He saw me running [on the sand] and came over and said, 'Why don't we take your motorcycle out on this highway and do some things to it and make it go a little faster?' We went out there on a back road, and I ran with another bike. I could stay even with him. We kept tinkering with mine, changing different things over a four-day period, and pretty soon I outran the other bike pretty bad. That helped me win the 200-mile bike race on the beach."

Yunick, a mechanical genius who also had a good eye for talented drivers, pushed Goldsmith into stock cars, and they returned to the beach and the tough 4.1-mile test with four wheels.

Goldsmith probably could have challenged for a Cup championship, but he never ran anything close to a full season. He finished fifth in points in 1966 despite running only twenty-one of the forty-nine races.

"It was difficult to get a car set up for both the beach and the highway," Goldsmith said. "And the highway was rough. The car wouldn't handle unless you had the right suspension. Smokey helped me with that quite a bit. We went out on a back road there about four miles north of Daytona and worked on different shocks, tire pressures, and suspensions. That's where we learned how to do it. And I had raced motorcycles there, so that helped."

Goldsmith outran Curtis Turner, the driver he later would classify as the toughest to beat, to win the beach-road course finale in a Pontiac carrying sponsorship from Yunick's famous "Best Damn Garage in Town."

Goldsmith won once in Cup in 1956, four times in 1957, once in 1958, and three times in 1966, his best season.

By the time Goldsmith, who also raced at Indianapolis Motor Speedway and in USAC stock cars, retired from competition in 1969 to concentrate on business interests, his home and office were filled with trophies from a spectrum of racing disciplines, including, oddly, one for a brief foray into harness racing.

At ninety-five years old, Goldsmith remains active. His office at the Griffith-Merrillville (Indiana) Airport (which he owns) contains some racing memorabilia, but his trophies were scattered to the winds over the years, some going to friends and relatives. "I had a truckload in here," he said. "I had to get rid of them."

CHAPTER 38

Jeff Burton

Texas Motor Speedway, Apr. 6, 1997

Jeff Burton emerged from the muck, mire, and controversy of one of the wildest weeks in NASCAR history to score his first victory in the Cup Series.

Texas Motor Speedway (TMS) opened in 1997 as track ownership titan Bruton Smith's latest brainchild, a huge auto-racing showplace rising out of the Texas landscape near Dallas and Fort Worth. As with many things in Texas, it was big and it was bold, and it promised dazzling racing for the NASCAR opener April 6.

Then it rained. And it rained again. And more rain fell. TMS parking lots turned into mush. Qualifying was canceled. Race day was a mucky mess, and incoming traffic issues were compounded by the closing of some parking lots.

Additionally, the track itself was trouble. Drivers complained about poor design in Turns One and Four, and some predicted calamity.

Calamity arrived. And quickly. A thirteen-car wreck occurred on the first lap, and ten cautions flew by day's end, eating seventy-three of the race's 334 laps.

At the end of a long, tense day, Burton was king of the soggy hill. He led the last fifty-eight laps and beat second-place Dale Jarrett to the checkered flag by 4.06 seconds, notching the first of his twenty-one Cup Series wins.

"When they designed the track, it was just not very well done, and it caught a lot of us off guard," Burton said. "They kind of advertised it as a sister track to Charlotte, and it was just a mess. The exit of Turn Four was really, really difficult. At the entrance to Turn One, the banking change was not done very well.

"It kind of makes it cool that I won my first race there on such a challenging weekend. I feel like you really had to get your head in the right place and approach that track differently than you had with other racetracks that were that big. We as a team did a good job of that."

The technical difficulties associated with running the right lines through Turns One and Four, especially in traffic, made competing on the new track a unique task, Burton said.

"You had to be real precise," he said. "You had to change your mindset a little bit. You couldn't just throw the race car around the track. In retrospect, we were just at the beginning of understanding that with new racetracks or with tracks that had just been paved the tire compound was so different to keep the tires lasting and the tires didn't drive very well. I think we were pointing our fingers at the track, and there

Jeff Burton recorded a remarkable accomplishment September 17, 2000, in the Dura Lube 300 at New Hampshire Motor Speedway. Burton led all three hundred laps—a notable oddity in NASCAR's modern era—in winning the race. The 300 was held under unusual circumstances, as all cars were fitted for engine restrictor plates as NASCAR reacted with caution to recent driver deaths at the 1.058-mile track. "People discount that win at Loudon because we had restrictor plates," Burton said. "Well, everybody had restrictor plates. We went to Milwaukee [a similar track] and tested. We busted our ass. We outworked everybody and won that race."

Jeff Burton won at Texas Motor Speedway in 1997, scoring his first Cup victory in the track's inaugural race.
DAVID GRIFFIN

were other contributing factors about which we were kind of ignorant at the time.

"It was challenging, though. We went there to test, and I drove a rental car before testing and almost hit the wall off Turn Four. I knew right then I was going to have to adjust as a driver to how I approached the track."

Late in the race, while racing Burton for the lead, Todd Bodine spun and hit the wall. Burton had clear sailing the rest of the way. Bodine had led the previous eight laps.

"The way I remember that is that I really don't think I ever hit him," Burton said. "I think it was all air. I got to him, and the cars didn't have a lot of grip. He started around. I don't think I touched him."

Fourteen drivers in the starting field of forty-three failed to finish the race, nine because of crashes.

After the TMS inaugural, the track was reconfigured to make running through the offending turns much smoother.

Burton would go on to become a weekly victory threat in the Cup Series. By career's end, he had driven for two of NASCAR's top teams—Roush Fenway Racing and Richard Childress Racing.

Before the breakthrough win, Burton had had twelve top-five finishes.

"We were running well, but one of the reasons we weren't winning is that we were a new team," Burton said. "We had a newer pit crew, and we weren't having great pit stops. We needed to be better. I needed to be better. I was making some mistakes late in races because I hadn't been in that situation a lot, and I was doing it against a different caliber of driver. But we had good pace. And we had [crew chief] Buddy Parrott. And Buddy Parrott wasn't going to let you get down or pout or look at the negatives. He was going to pick you up and move you forward.

When safety issues became front and center for NASCAR, Burton took an active role in analysis and testing to improve conditions in car cockpits and in the implementation of SAFER barriers on track walls. Somewhere along the way, he picked up the nickname "Mayor" in the garage area.

"The idea was that we're going to prove to the world we can do this. It was sort of an us-against-the-world thing."

And the world finished second. At least in a memorable week in Texas.

CHAPTER 39

Tiny Lund

Daytona (FL) International Speedway, Feb. 24, 1963

Not even the most creative Hollywood script writer would consider a storyline this schmaltzy: an unemployed, semi-obscure racing driver helps rescue an injured colleague from almost certain death in a fiery accident; from a nearby hospital, the injured driver recommends the hero to drive his car in the year's most important race; against all odds, the unknown hero becomes an overnight sensation by winning the Daytona 500 in remarkable fashion.

It would all sound unimaginable if it hadn't truly happened in Daytona Beach in February of 1963. It unfolded like this:

Dwayne "Tiny" Lund was six foot five and about 260 pounds when NASCAR arrived at Daytona International Speedway that year. The Iowa native and Korean War veteran had raced motorcycles, sprint cars, and midgets in the Midwest before coming south in the mid-1950s to try his hand at this new Bill France–created stock car series. As a sideline, he ran a popular freshwater fishing camp near his new hometown of Cross, in the Lowcountry of South Carolina.

Fishing was good, but racing was a frustrating struggle. Lund was good enough to support himself and his family with occasional NASCAR Cup Series rides, but his prospects for long-term stardom and financial stability seemed slim. Everyone in racing liked him—his sense of humor was contagious; he always seemed in a good mood; his heart was as big as the Daytona infield—but racing just part-time was stressful. Almost penniless but desperate for work, the ever-hopeful Lund went to Daytona Beach for Speed Week 1963.

That's when fate stepped in to change his life forever.

Ten days before the 500, during practice for a sports car race, Marvin Panch flipped his 7-litre Ford/Maserati entering Turn Four. Within moments Lund, Ernie Gahan, Bill Wimble, Jerry Raborn, and Steve Petrasek sprinted to the scene. After one effort failed, the men lifted the car so Lund could yank Panch from the cockpit. The Daytona Beach resident and 1961 Daytona 500 winner suffered injuries and burns that immediately sidelined him from the upcoming five-hundred-miler.

"I remember quite a bit of the accident," Panch told *Daytona Beach News-Journal* columnist Ken Willis in 2013. (At eighty-nine, Panch died on New Year's Eve of 2015). "Let me tell you, when you're trapped in the car and can't get out, everything I'd done bad in my life flashed in front of me. When someone tells you that, believe 'em because it's true. Everything goes through your mind at a thousand miles an hour. It's a bad feeling."

As for the rescue itself: "The car was upside down and I couldn't get out," Panch recalled. (The gull-wing doors were jammed shut). "They lifted it just enough for me to start getting out, then the gas tank blew and they had to drop it. But I could hear Steve yelling, 'He's still kicking' [meaning Panch was alive]. They came back and lifted it again and Tiny grabbed me by the leg and pulled me out. It's obvious that if it wasn't for them I wouldn't be talking to you now." (Later, the Carnegie Foundation honored the five rescuers with medals for heroism).

Wood Brothers Racing co-founder Leonard Wood expanded on the rescue. "Marvin told me later, 'I was just about ready to take a breath of flame to put myself out of my misery,'" Wood said. "He said, 'I didn't want to be burned alive.' Right after that Tiny reached back in the car and pulled him out. They for sure saved him."

During his recovery in a nearby hospital, Panch asked the Wood brothers to give Lund his ride for the 500. "It was already my brother's [Glen] and my decision to use Tiny because we thought he was the best man available," Leonard Wood said. "We used to race against him and he was one tough competitor."

On race weekend, Lund qualified fourth, was sixth in his one-hundred-mile heat race, and started twelfth. Knowing they couldn't win on raw speed, the team gambled with an unorthodox strategy: run all five hundred miles on one set of Firestone tires and with one fewer pit stop. Lund drafted well and was close on fuel when he took his first NASCAR checkered flag by an astonishing twenty-four seconds ahead of rookie Fred Lorenzen. Lund led only seventeen laps, including the final eight after Ned Jarrett pitted for fuel at lap 192.

"Nobody had ever run five hundred miles on one set of tires," Leonard Wood explained. "I thought we could because I built my own spindles that reduced tire roll and made them wear evenly across the footprint. Nobody else could have done what we did because they were wearing out their tires. And our stops were quicker because we weren't changing tires. We kept going a few laps more than everybody else between stops, which let us make one fewer stop."

An excellent fisherman, Lund made the catch of his life in January 1963, pulling a South Carolina record striped bass weighing fifty-five pounds from Lake Moultrie. The record stood for thirty years.

If this were a G-rated Disney movie, Lund would have ridden that storybook victory to a long and rewarding career. Granted, he won four more short-track races, but never again enjoyed the thrill of a major superspeedway victory. His greatest success came in the lower-level Grand American series, where he won the 1968 GA title in Bud Moore–prepared Cougars and the 1970–1971 titles in Camaros with owner Ronnie Hopkins.

Overall, he won 41 of 109 starts, mostly on short tracks that didn't get major races. He won the renamed 1973 "Grand National East" title with three poles and five victories (plus eleven top fives and fifteen top tens) in twenty-five starts.

Ironically, Lund died in 1975 at Talladega Superspeedway in a race he shouldn't have been in.

Mostly retired for the previous few seasons, Lund had accepted a one-off ride in the No. 26 Dodge from A. J. King. Lund didn't qualify, but advanced as first alternate when Grant Adcox withdrew after his crew chief died of a heart attack before the race. After a weeklong weather delay, Lund made only six laps before suffering fatal injuries in a massive backstretch accident. He was forty-five and left behind a wife, Wanda, and son, Christopher.

CHAPTER 40

Martin Truex Jr.

Dover (DE) International Speedway, June 4, 2007

Watching Atlantic Ocean waves roll to increasingly scary heights from the bow of a ninety-six-foot clam boat, Martin Truex Jr. figured the view through the windshield of a race car was fine, indeed.

Because his father owns a seafood business, Truex Jr. grew up on boats. As a teenager, he worked long hours at sea. None of it was fun, he remembers, but one journey stands out.

"We hit a bad storm coming home," he said. "All the drawers were flying out. All the drawers had come out of all the cabinets in the galley. The refrigerator door had flung open, crap flying everywhere. I remember climbing up the stairs, hanging on to the railing, looking out and saying, 'Holy hell, this is bad.' I mean, it was nothing but white as far as you could see. It was like fourteen-foot swells we were in.

"I figured out real quick that I ought to figure out how to be good at this racing thing because I didn't want to be working on these boats the rest of my life."

Two-hundred-mile-per-hour laps at Daytona? Five hundred grueling laps at Bristol? A long, sweaty day at Darlington? Bring it on, thought Truex, who had mixed some short-track racing in the Northeast into his time working for his father. He described clam boat work

Martin Truex Jr. gave up a career working on clam boats to race—and win—in NASCAR. *David Griffin*

as "dirty, stinky, cold, sweaty" and worked every angle to avoid becoming a clam boat captain. Racing was the answer.

Fast forward to June 4, 2007, and Truex completed the task of turning toward racing and making it work. In his second full season in the Cup Series, driving for Dale Earnhardt Inc., then one of racing's top teams, he joined the list of Cup winners by dominating the Autism Speaks 400 at Dover, Delaware.

When he won the 2017 Cup championship, Truex became the first New Jersey native to claim NASCAR's top title.

Among those celebrating was his father, Martin Truex Sr., whose SeaWatch International company has dozens of boats and seven hundred employees. He said his son "fit right in" on his first working boat run. "He had been around it on the docks and all prior to going out," he said. "He didn't like it, but it made him a better race car driver. I wanted him to know what work was about. And he did well. Martin has succeeded at anything he's ever done because he puts one hundred percent into it."

When Truex finally won, he left no questions unanswered. He led 216 of the 500 laps, including the final fifty-four, and won by 7.35 seconds over Ryan Newman. It seemed almost easy, but, of course, it wasn't.

The Dover weekend began with Truex and his team climbing a mountain of sorts.

"In qualifying practice we were way off," Truex remembered. "I said, 'We need to change something big.' We changed a whole bunch of stuff in the front-end geometry, changed the right front spindle, threw a bunch of stuff at it.

"Then when I started the final practice, I thought, 'Holy crap. This thing is awesome.'"

And it was. On a fast, tough track that tends to eat race cars and makes runaway victories rare, Truex sailed home with few worries.

Truex scored his first Cup win on a day that otherwise was a dark one in the world of NASCAR. Bill France Jr., the organization's long-time chairman and architect of the sport's move to national status, died that day after a long battle with cancer.

"It was back in those days when so much about the car [the oddly configured Car of Tomorrow] was new, and you could find something," he said. "And we did. It was incredible."

For the son of a fisherman, it seemed entirely appropriate that Truex screamed "Holy mackerel!" into his team radio after crossing the checkered flag.

He had landed the big one.

"The first win makes you think at first, 'What just happened?'" Truex said. "You're just so damn happy. And it was a little bit of a relief because it took a year and whatever to get it."

Although delayed in arriving, Truex's Cup success was not unexpected. He had won two Nationwide (later Xfinity) Series titles in Dale Earnhardt Jr.'s team cars in 2004 and 2005. At the end of the 2006 Cup season, searching for Cup win No. 1, he finished second to Greg Biffle in the final race at Homestead, Florida.

He scored his first extended run of success with Furniture Row Racing, winning a race in 2015 and advancing to the championship final four that season and in 2016. The fortunes of the Denver, Colorado–based team peaked in 2017 as Truex won eight races, including four of the final ten, and took home the Cup championship.

A year later, Furniture Row owner Barney Visser left the sport, and Truex moved on to Joe Gibbs Racing, where he has continued to contend for wins and championships.

CHAPTER 41

Bubba Wallace

Talladega (AL) Superspeedway, Oct. 4, 2021

B ubba Wallace scored his first NASCAR Cup Series win while sitting atop a pit box, shielded from the weather, running at 0 miles per hour.

No matter.

The moment would have been grander if Wallace had made a daring pass in the final turn on the final lap to win the YellaWood 500 at Talladega Superspeedway, but that's a minor quibble that the history books will ignore.

It's right there in black and white—in this case, it's especially in black and white. Wallace won at Talladega in October 2021 against all of the best drivers NASCAR could attract, and his name was added to the Pettys and Pearsons and Waltrips and Johnsons and all the others who reached the top rung of their sport.

In Wallace's case, the win in the rain-shortened race (117 of 188 laps completed) held additional importance beyond being the first victory for the Alabama driver. The win was only the second by a Black driver in Cup history—and the first since Wendell Scott, a struggling but determined privateer from Virginia, won on a tiny track in Jacksonville, Florida in 1963.

Bubba Wallace
added his name to
the Cup winners
list with a victory
at Talladega
Superspeedway
in 2021.
DAVID GRIFFIN

When persistent rain forced the Talladega race to be called, Wallace ran into the arms of his 23XI Racing teammates, and a celebration that had been anticipated since Wallace broke into the Cup series in 2017 was on.

Wallace took the lead from Kurt Busch on lap 113 as threatening skies made it likely that the race would be red-flagged and possibly end short of the full distance. He was still in front on lap 117 when a four-car wreck on the backstretch brought out the caution flag. Rain then pounded the track, bringing out the red flag.

Members of the 23XI team huddled on and around its pit box on pit road to wait for the skies to clear or for NASCAR to make the race official. After about forty-five minutes, the call to end the race at 117 laps was made, and Wallace stepped into history.

Wallace, who had won races in the Camping World Truck Series, made his move into Cup racing when Aric Almirola, driving for Richard Petty Motorsports, was injured during the 2017 season. RPM called on Wallace as a fill-in for four races, and those runs led the team to sign Wallace full-time for 2018 after Almirola moved on.

"This is for all those kids out there that want to have an opportunity in whatever they want to achieve and be the best at whatever they want to do," Wallace said. "You're going to go through a lot of bullshit, but you've always got to stick true to your path and not let the nonsense get to you.

"Stay strong, stay humble, stay hungry. There have been plenty of times that I wanted to give up, but you surround yourself with the right people, and it's moments like this that you appreciate. It's a huge weight lifted off my shoulders."

Bubba Wallace on track at Atlanta Motor Speedway.
David Griffin

Wallace won four days short of his twenty-eighth birthday. The victory was the first for 23XI Racing, owned by Cup driver Denny Hamlin and former basketball superstar Michael Jordan.

Among the many lining up to congratulate Wallace was fellow driver Ryan Blaney, his best friend in the garage area. He gave Wallace a long hug on pit road after the race.

"It shows that maybe someone who is not as common in the sport, being a person of color, can come in and be a success in the sport," Blaney said. "I hope it opens a lot of kids' eyes to try out racing. They can see the success that Bubba has and say, 'Man, I want to be just like him.' There are kids like that all over the world. I think this is big not only for Bubba but for the sport and for kids who've looked up to him for a long time."

Social media exploded with both congratulations and criticism after Wallace's win. There were suggestions that NASCAR ended the race early to "give" the win to Wallace and that the victory really didn't count because the race was rain-shortened, this despite the fact that many other NASCAR wins have been scored in events shortened by weather. As a key point, Wallace raced hard over the final green-flag laps to get and keep the lead.

Hamlin, after celebrating with his winning driver, said both he and Wallace had been the targets of social media abuse. "Those people just need to grow up, honestly, appreciate the accomplishment that the kid just had," Hamlin said. "I think people just have a microscope on him because they want to be critical. They just are haters."

The win came with a big slice of irony. In 2020, at the same track, Wallace was the center of attention after a rope shaped into a noose

Wallace has often said that he races in the tire tracks of Wendell Scott, the Cup Series's first Black winner, but that he focuses on performance, not the past. "For sure, I'm carrying that banner," he said. "A small part carries him with me, but I don't put that in the forefront. For me, it's just to go out and get through practice, qualifying and the race."

was left in his team's garage area, leading to an FBI investigation amid concern he was being targeted as part of a hate crime. The investigation determined that the rope had been tied in that fashion before the beginning of the race weekend, meaning it could not have been specifically aimed at Wallace or his team.

CHAPTER 42

Harry Gant

Martinsville (VA) Speedway, Apr. 25, 1982

Harry Gant never let his "0-fer" NASCAR Cup Series losing streak bother him. He was generally upbeat and optimistic, ever hopeful that his next start would be the one that took him to victory lane. He never publicly complained about struggling to win at the Cup level.

That was the situation when "Hard-Luck Harry" and his No. 33 Skoal Bandit team arrived at Martinsville Speedway late in April of 1982. A fan favorite after years on regional weekly tracks, the forty-two-year-old North Carolinian was considered better than his zero for 107 Cup record might suggest.

Far better, in fact.

By then in his career, Gant had ten second-place finishes. Some had been heartbreaking last-lap losses; others had been humiliating routs. His first runner-up was by a split-second in April 1980 at North Wilkesboro. Later that season, he was second at Dover and Rockingham. He was second a frustrating seven more times in 1981, including consecutive weekends in Michigan and Daytona Beach.

But at least Gant wasn't losing to backmarkers. Those three second-place finishes in 1980 were to future Hall of Fame superstars Richard Petty, Darrell Waltrip, and Cale Yarborough. The next year he lost

Harry Gant rolled into the Cup Series late in his career but enjoyed a string of success in the Skoal Bandit cars. *JERRY HAISLIP / BRH ARCHIVES*

twice each to Yarborough, Waltrip, and Bobby Allison, and once to Benny Parsons. (Again . . . all Hall of Famers and champions.) Several losses were by a car-length and several others were under caution.

All the while, Gant kept any frustrations to himself. "He didn't let it show," said veteran crew chief Travis Carter. "He was performing better than at any time in his career. I think he'd get a little upset now and then, but I kept reminding him—'Let me tell you about this business: run well long enough and you're going to win. You have to have good speed and be competitive before you can win.'

"Harry managed it well. He didn't feel pressured to win. [Team co-owner] Hal Needham was thrilled with the way we were running. We were getting great press and good TV coverage. We just had a lot of little issues—a flat tire at the wrong time. Stuff like that."

At fifty-two years and 219 days, Gant was the oldest Cup
winner when he won at Michigan in August 1992, and at
forty-two years and 105 days, he was NASCAR's oldest
driver to get his first Cup victory. He's eighty-two now,
and those records remain.

Nothing went insurmountably wrong on that April day in Martinsville.
Lapped twice and a non-factor much of the race, Gant made up the deficits
and ran down the leaders under green. "I was crying when I took the checkered," he admitted afterward. "Can you believe that? After thirteen hundred
races [in many series and with untold victories], I was crying because this
one is so special. This is the best feeling I've ever had in racing."

The Skoal Bandit
sponsorship of
Harry Gant was
one of the most
successful in the
history of NASCAR.
Dick Conway

Most in the crowd of thirty thousand were thrilled for Gant, Carter, and Needham. As one series-watcher chronicled: *"Along pit road, the hardened fraternity of mechanics and owners cheered him. Regardless of the past or the future, this was a special moment in stock car racing, an emotional moment when a hard-working, well-behaved, clean-driving, popular gentleman finally got what he so richly deserved. Virtually everyone in the place stood to salute him. Even fans of NASCAR's long-established stars—Petty, the Allisons, Waltrip, Baker, Parsons, Earnhardt, etc.—set aside their one-man loyalty for the moment and joined Gant's legion of fans. They waved their caps, jackets, beer cans, and programs as he took a teary victory lap."*

It had been a long time coming.

Gant's career began with countless street races in western North Carolina. He went legit in 1963, racing a Hobby Class car at Hickory in North Carolina. He advanced to the faster and more sophisticated Late Models, then briefly raced in NASCAR's Grand National East series. He made the first of his 474 Cup starts in October 1973 at Charlotte for owner Junie Donlavey.

He spent the next few years getting occasional Cup rides while concentrating on major Late Model shows in the South and along the Eastern Seaboard. He won hundreds of weekly short-track races—as usual, stats are somewhat sketchy—and several track championships.

In 1979, at the relatively advanced age of thirty-nine, Gant went full-time Cup racing for owners Kennie Childers and Jack Beebe. He spent two-plus seasons with their mediocre teams before signing on for 1982–1988 with movie stuntman Needham and Hollywood star Burt Reynolds. With Carter atop the pit box, the team won ten poles and nine races in seven years together. Gant spent the last six years of his career (1989–1994) with Richard and Leo Jackson, winning seven more poles and nine more races. At fifty-four, after the 1994 season,

Two other notables were in Gant's 1979 Rookie of the Year (ROTY) class: future multi-time champions and NASCAR Hall of Famers Dale Earnhardt (the ROTY winner) and Terry Labonte.

Harry Gant became
"Mr. September" after
scoring four straight
Cup victories in
September 1991.
DICK CONWAY

Gant retired, content with his career record that included eight top-ten points seasons.

He ended his zero for 107 losing streak on a bright Sunday afternoon at Martinsville. He qualified third behind Terry Labonte and Parsons, then led three times for 167 laps, including the final 144. He won by more than a lap over Butch Lindley, a popular and well-respected friendly rival from their Late Model barnstorming days.

Ironically, Gant may have benefited from contact with Lindley at lap 318 of 500. They were second-third behind Waltrip when they got together in Turn Two. Lindley looped from contact and Gant suffered major right-front and front-end damage. Ironically, the front-end damage created openings for more fresh air to his car's front brakes. That proved a huge late-race advantage on a hot day at the accelerate-and-brake track.

"Butch and Harry were running good," Carter recalled. "When they got tangled, Harry's front end got beat up. He thought the way to run good at Martinsville was to keep the brakes cool. [After the incident,] he had air flowing everywhere over the front end and onto the brakes. He was thrilled to death with that. He thought that was how he could win."

Perhaps surprisingly, there wasn't a huge post-race celebration. "We didn't have great elation after winning," Carter said. "It was more like a load off our shoulders. Harry probably had a big grin, but he was kind of even-keeled. [Winning] was what people expected of us. We'd done our job and it was time to go home and get ready for Talladega. You know . . . the cycle that never ends."

CHAPTER 43

Tim Flock

Charlotte (NC) Speedway, Apr. 2, 1950

C ompared to the rest of his racing life, Tim Flock's first NASCAR Cup Series win was relatively nondescript.

It occurred at the three-quarter-mile Charlotte (North Carolina) Speedway on April 2, 1950, in NASCAR's second Cup season. The Charlotte track, long defunct, had staged the very first race in Bill France's new stock car series the previous year.

Driving a 1949 Lincoln, Flock was the class of a twenty-five-car field in the 1950 race. He won by about a half-lap over his brother, Bob, leading the last 153 of 200 laps.

A certified pioneer of the sport—he raced five times in 1949, Cup's inaugural season, and in NASCAR Modifieds prior to that year—Flock won thirty-nine Cup races over a career that spanned thirteen years. He won two Cup championships (1952 and 1955) and was inducted into the NASCAR Hall of Fame in 2014.

But the Flock story is about so much more than the wins and the associated numbers. It is a great American story.

Tim was the youngest of ten children in a family of daredevils. One or more members of the extended family drove race cars, walked tightropes, performed as a wing-walker at airplane shows, raced speed-boats, and hauled illegal booze through Georgia backwoods.

And, not to be forgotten, one of them—that would be Tim—drove eight Cup races with a monkey—yes, a monkey—as passenger and "co-pilot." Jocko Flocko rode with Flock in at least eight races (they shared one win) before what was mostly a publicity stunt ended when Jocko escaped his seat during a race in Raleigh, North Carolina, and went just a bit crazy while Flock struggled to get to the pits to unload his disturbed passenger.

So, yes, the Flocks were unique—one of the first families of American auto racing and one with tales that stretch the bounds of credulity. The vast majority are true, for the 1950s produced some of the bravest and most daring of all race car drivers, men (and the occasional woman) who drove fast and hard to put biscuits on the family table the next week.

The Flock family produced four racers—Tim, brothers Bob and Fonty, and Ethel, their sister. This allowed the family to claim a NASCAR first that is likely never to be repeated—three brothers and one sister competing in the same race.

Tim, regarded as one of the smoothest drivers in NASCAR history, was easily the most accomplished racer in the family, but Fonty scored nineteen Cup wins and Bob won four times. Ethel didn't win in Cup, but in the Daytona beach-road course race in 1949, Cup's first season, she finished eleventh, ahead of Fonty (nineteenth) and Bob (twenty-second). Tim was second to race-winner Red Byron.

Flock won the Daytona beach-road course race in 1956 despite running into a flock (yes, Flock hit a flock) of seagulls along the beach part of the course and finding his vision quite limited by the mess on the windshield. He leaned from the car window while roaring down the beach and cleaned the windshield with a brush. Flock held on to win the race, one that ended a bit early because the Atlantic Ocean was roaring toward high tide.

Bob, by the way, was targeted as a moonshine runner by Atlanta area police. He showed up for a race at Lakewood Speedway near the city and was spotted by cops. He jumped in his car, zoomed around the track, broke through a fence, and was gone in a flash.

Just another crazy but true Flock tale.

Tim, who became a popular ambassador for Charlotte Motor Speedway after he left driving in 1961, produced one of the most remarkable seasons in Cup history. In 1955, on the way to winning his second championship in one of team owner Carl Kiekhaefer's legendary Chrysler 300s, he scored eighteen victories, a record that stood until Richard Petty logged twenty-seven wins in 1967.

Flock was a runaway train that year. He won across the continent, scoring at Syracuse, New York, and at San Mateo, California. He won two races at the treacherous Langhorne track in Pennsylvania. He won three straight races near the start of the season and scored six victories at tracks in the Carolinas.

Flock's first Cup title, in 1952, was sealed under unusual circumstances. He and dirt-track star Herb Thomas, a farmer who stumbled into racing almost by chance, had battled for the point lead all season. Thomas won the season finale at West Palm Beach, Florida, but Flock scored enough points to win the championship. Thirty-six laps from the finish, his Hudson hit the wall and flipped onto its roof before sliding down the frontstretch. "I bet I'm the only driver who ever won a championship on his head," Flock said afterward.

"The Flocks had different personalities and different driving styles," said long-time promoter Humpy Wheeler. "Tim was probably the smoothest of them. He was one of the greatest drivers in history."

Flock's career was not without controversy.

Flock scored his first victory as a teenager. It wasn't in a race car. He picked up a yo-yo as a kid and became proficient at spinning tricks. He entered a competition and was crowned the Yo-Yo King of Atlanta.

In 1950, Flock ran for both the NASCAR Cup and Modified titles. He won the Modified title, but that championship was nullified by NASCAR president Bill France, who penalized Flock for running in a non-NASCAR-sanctioned event. France kept a tight rein on drivers who had committed to racing under the NASCAR emblem.

A much bigger issue arose in 1961. Flock joined NASCAR superstar Curtis Turner in trying to form a drivers union. France ruled both drivers ineligible for life. They later were reinstated, but Flock didn't run another race.

CHAPTER 44

Junior Johnson

Hickory (NC) Speedway, May 7, 1955

Junior Johnson's career as a NASCAR Cup Series driver was winding down as David Pearson's was accelerating.

They met in a memorable battle for the win on September 11, 1964, at Hickory (North Carolina) Speedway, then a 0.4-mile dirt track. Pearson led the first twenty-one laps before Johnson bulled his way in front for the next forty-three.

"To outrun Junior there was something," Pearson remembered years later. "After lap after lap, I finally got around him. He followed me real close, hounding me, trying to get me to overdrive and get in the wall. I just kept cutting across coming off the second turn and slinging mud in his radiator. Got his old car running hot."

Johnson parked at lap eighty-nine, his car overheating. Pearson had passed him on lap sixty-five for the lead and never looked back, winning the 250-lap race by three laps over Larry Thomas.

In those days, beating Junior Johnson on a dirt track was a big deal. Competitors often needed a smart, slick move like Pearson's to deny Johnson, a driver from the old-school mold who squeezed engines, tires, and frames for all they were worth. For Johnson, it often was win or crash. There was no middle ground.

As both a driver and team owner, Junior Johnson attracted fans who favored his hard-charging style. *Dick Conway*

From 1958 to 1965, Johnson scored forty-five of his career-total fifty wins. He was a force of nature, one of the pioneer drivers who raced with no evident sign of fear, living purely on the edge.

"You always had to wonder if the car would hold up under him," said Dale Inman, crew chief for driver Richard Petty, who said he often watched Johnson drive with amazement. "That's the way he was. There were no ifs, ands, or buts about it. He drove the car unmercifully."

Although Johnson won races with regularity, he never won a Cup driving championship, clear evidence of his win-races-at-all-costs approach. He had no love for "points" racing.

Johnny Allen raced often against Johnson. "Crawford Clements was Junior's crew chief in the early 1960s," Allen said. "They started having problems, falling out of races after leading because something would break. Crawford said it was Junior, said he would break an anvil, that nobody could keep a car under him." Johnson eventually quit the team.

NASCAR historian Buz McKim said Johnson was similar to Curtis Turner, another star of NASCAR's early years. "They just didn't care," he said. "They were reckless. They were really kind of scary crazy."

Robert Glenn Johnson Jr. was working the ground of the Johnson family farm behind a mule when his older brother, L. P., offered him the chance to drive a race car. Junior knew almost nothing about racing, but he had driven fast cars making moonshine deliveries from the Johnson family's other "business" along Carolina backroads, so he hesitated only a moment before heading to the track. He needed a minute—he had been plowing barefooted, so he figured he needed to head to the house to get shoes to race.

"When I got into racing, I already had the experience I needed," Johnson said years later. "I didn't have to learn how to drive fast. I already knew how to do it."

He arrived in Cup racing in 1953 at the age of twenty-two. He won on tracks across the country, totaling fifty victories before retiring in 1966 and moving toward team ownership, where he was even more successful than in his driving days.

Johnson was an easy pick for the first class of the NASCAR Hall of Fame. He drove from the backwoods of western North Carolina to the boardrooms of major corporations and into the hearts of thousands of race fans who liked their drivers to talk slow and run fast.

Johnson's life might have moved in another direction if not for a tractor accident on the family farm when he was fourteen. He had drawn considerable attention pitching for local baseball teams but broke his arm in the accident. "I dreamed of playing for the New York Yankees," he said.

Junior Johnson built a racing empire in the foothills of the Brushy Mountains in North Carolina.
DICK CONWAY

"I had hauled moonshine pretty much since I was about fifteen," Johnson said. "I was very talented with a car compared to most of the guys I grew up with. I had probably more nerve than they had.

"That sort of set the stage for me starting to get into it. Now and then, somebody would call me and want me to go drive their race car for them. I did that for a few years and kept working my way up. The first thing you know, I was in it full-time."

In 1955, Johnson notched his first Cup victory at Hickory, a bedrock NASCAR track and a proving ground for many Carolinas drivers over the years. Johnson led the final twenty-nine of two hundred laps, winning the race under caution over second-place Tim Flock, another pioneer legend.

Although Johnson was a titan on NASCAR's short tracks, he also loved the runaway speeds of the bigger tracks. He won the 1960 Daytona 500, the second 500 at the then-new giant Daytona International Speedway, and is widely credited with "discovering" the phenomenon of stock car drafting at the high-speed track. Despite having a slower car, he used the pulling effect of cars in front of him to slip through the field and emerge victorious.

Johnson gained fame beyond the usual context of a NASCAR racer when celebrated writer Tom Wolfe, one of the stars of the journalism field of the era, made him the center of a March 1965 article in *Esquire* magazine. The story—titled "Junior Johnson is the Last American Hero—

The Johnson family's moonshine business slowed Johnson's driving career. He was arrested at one of the family's stills in 1956 and eventually served eleven months in federal prison in Ohio.

Yes!"—described the rise of Johnson, his natural habitat in the Brushy Mountains of western North Carolina, and the attraction of stock car racing to the thousands who streamed into North Wilkesboro Speedway to watch him run. Wolfe's piece is respected as one of the greatest stories in sports journalism and served to give NASCAR, still an infant in the world of sports leagues, a more visible national profile.

Johnson won thirteen times in 1965 then decided abruptly to retire the next year.

"I said I had had enough of it and that I had other things I needed to do, and just walked away from it," he said.

He came back as a car owner and excelled, winning Cup championships with drivers Cale Yarborough (1976, 1977, 1978) and Darrell Waltrip (1981, 1982, and 1985).

Johnson operated a huge cattle farm on his property in Hamptonville, North Carolina. He built a mansion-type residence near his childhood home but moved to a residential neighborhood in Charlotte, North Carolina, as his life slowed in later years. He died in 2019.

"I guess I had three careers in my life—moonshining, driving, car owning," Johnson said. "I think I enjoyed the moonshining better than any of them. I don't know why. I guess it was the youth side of it. You never forget what you do as a kid."

CHAPTER 45

Matt Kenseth

Charlotte (NC) Motor Speedway, May 28, 2000

The road to Matt Kenseth's first NASCAR Cup victory runs directly through the story of his first Xfinity Series win, so we must start there, too.

Kenseth and crew chief Robbie Reiser planned for the 1998 Xfinity season to be their first full-time in NASCAR's second-level series, with Kenseth driving cars owned by the Reiser family. Kenseth opened the year with a strong sixth-place finish at Daytona International Speedway.

The second race was scheduled at North Carolina Motor Speedway in Rockingham. A promised sponsorship deal fell through, but, as a gesture of thanks for Lycos's sponsorship at Daytona, the team kept Lycos decals on the car for the second race.

The 200-miler ended with high drama. Tony Stewart held the lead on the last lap, but Kenseth passed him for first in the final turn and won by 0.092 of a second. It was one of the tightest finishes of the NASCAR season. Let Kenseth describe what he called "the coolest ending for me for a race ever."

"Back then, there was a certain way you went into the turn at Rockingham so that you grabbed the track with the left front and the car sort of hooked and pivoted perfectly," Kenseth said. "Tony didn't miss that,

Perhaps NASCAR's most understated champion, Matt Kenseth drove a Jack Roush–owned Ford to his first Cup victory. *DAVID GRIFFIN*

but his car didn't hook right. Mine hooked it just right so that I could floor it. I ran up toward him, about six inches to his left, made him a little loose and barely touched him and got underneath him.

"It's probably the most exciting race I've ever run."

Lycos, which had planned to sponsor Kenseth for only the season opener at Daytona, came on board for the rest of the season, rejoining what had become a winning team.

"That saved the season for me, the Reiser family, and the team," Kenseth said. "It was an unbelievable day that changed all of our lives in a way. It gave us that ray of confidence that we could do it."

There was carryover from the Rockingham breakthrough. Kenseth also won races at Pikes Peak and Dover and finished a strong second to his friend, Dale Earnhardt Jr., in series points.

Success at NASCAR's No. 2 level vaulted Kenseth into the Cup Series, and his first full year there—2000—produced his first win.

It came as a bit of a surprise in the Coca-Cola 600, the season's longest race. The 2000 race was Kenseth's first in the marathon, and, even stranger, it would be the only win of his long career in the Charlotte Motor Speedway event.

The four-hour, twelve-minute race seemed to belong to Earnhardt Jr. He led 175 laps, including large chunks of laps in a row, but his Chevrolet faded badly over the closing miles after a four-tire change, leaving Kenseth and Bobby Labonte to race for the win.

Kenseth passed Labonte with twenty-six laps to go and won by 0.573 of a second. "Once I ran Bobby down and passed him, I wasn't worried about him catching up," he said. "I knew I had a faster car on that run."

Only eighteen races into his Cup career, Kenseth had his first victory lane.

"Moving up to Cup was a big step," said Kenseth, a Wisconsin native whose strong runs on Midwestern short tracks had impressed the right people, including his forever friend Mark Martin. "I was racing against all the guys I had watched on TV or had watched practice on the track on Saturdays when I was there for a Busch [later Xfinity] race.

"To be on the same track with them—racing against Rusty Wallace and Mark Martin and Dale Earnhardt—seemed like a really big deal. To beat them in one of the biggest races of the year was a huge accomplishment and a huge confidence boost for me."

Kenseth said he and his team celebrated the Charlotte win late into that night. Then they moved on to the next item on the list—the next race.

"Obviously, the more success you have, it leads to financial rewards down the road,"

> Kenseth left racing with a pair of Daytona 500 victories, a Cup championship, and the Cup Rookie of the Year award. He drove for team owners Jack Roush and Joe Gibbs and later briefly for Chip Ganassi.

he said. "But, in the moment, it didn't really change anything. We got to enjoy it for four or five days, but it was the middle of the season and we went on to the next one. I enjoyed it and had a ton of fun, but I didn't sit and dwell on wins. In fact, I probably dwelled on losses more."

Kenseth won five Cup races for team owner Jack Roush two years later, and, in 2003, finished in the top ten in twenty-five of the season's thirty-six races to win his only Cup championship. Kenseth won only one race that year, but his amazing consistency gave him the championship.

NASCAR changed its point system the next season, the first step in what eventually would become a playoff structure, writing an end to the "points racing" style that had been so rewarding to consistent drivers like Kenseth.

Kenseth totaled thirty-nine Cup victories over a twenty-two-year career.

"I really had only one goal I remember making in racing," he said. "I started racing when I was sixteen, and I remember thinking after a year or two, 'Man, I want to figure out how to race for a living so I don't have to have a normal job.'

"Working on race cars and driving them was really all I wanted to do. That's where my passion was. I certainly accomplished that goal, and the rest exceeded anything I could have dreamed about. The rest was not something that seemed realistic."

Kenseth's racing has not been limited to four wheels. He has run in marathons and participated in long-distance bicycle competition.

CHAPTER 46

Michael Waltrip

Daytona (FL) International Speedway, Feb. 18, 2001

What should have been the *best* day of Michael Waltrip's racing life turned into the *worst*. His joy at winning the 2001 Daytona 500 vanished with the news that Dale Earnhardt had died just as Waltrip was winning the sport's biggest event at Daytona International Speedway.

After breaking his zero for 462 NASCAR Cup Series drought dating to 1985, the "other" Waltrip could celebrate for barely a half hour. The death of the seven-time champion and his team owner just as Waltrip was winning the 500 made everything else meaningless.

That Sunday morning in Daytona Beach had started like so many others during his career. Waltrip hung out in his motorhome, fulfilled some "meet-and-greet" obligations, chatted with Earnhardt and teammates Dale Earnhardt Jr. and Steve Park, and visited with fans in the paddock and on pit road. Routine.

During the race he dutifully followed his boss's game plan. The three Dale Earnhardt Inc. cars were to draft and help each other whenever possible. Be patient and calculating, Earnhardt had told them, because their Chevrolets were capable of winning. Despite driving for another team, Earnhardt assured his drivers that he had their backs. Reassuring.

Waltrip ran well enough to lead laps 102–103, then 167–168, and 171–176. When he took the point from Earnhardt Jr. at lap 184, he was there the final sixteen laps. As he took his first checkered flag, third-running Earnhardt was crashing with Sterling Marlin, Ken Schrader, and the outside Turn Four wall. Many claim that Earnhardt was blocking so Waltrip and Earnhardt Jr. could get away; others say they were so far gone that he was blocking to ensure third for himself. In either case . . . worrisome.

It was confirmed at a nearby hospital that Earnhardt was unresponsive when rescue and medical teams reached the accident scene. (Schrader suspected the worst after looking into Earnhardt's cockpit.) A hospital statement said Earnhardt had died from a basilar skull fracture. He had little chance regardless of how quickly the ambulance got him to the hospital.

At first, Waltrip was told only that Earnhardt had crashed approaching the checkered flag. With no apparent reason not to, the first-time winner went to victory lane for a raucous celebration. He did the usual media/radio/TV interviews while growing concerned that Earnhardt wasn't there to celebrate with the team. It was perhaps a half hour later when he was told the truth.

"The worst day of my life," is how he described that February 18th. "It went from the best day to the worst." Later, in a wide-ranging interview, he added: "I think everything happens for a reason. If I could change history, the hug I would have gotten from Dale after the race would have been the best hug I'd ever had."

Now sixty, well known, and generally embraced as a harmless television personality, Waltrip was asked which comes to mind first when that day is mentioned, his victory or Earnhardt's death?

"It's definitely Dale," he said without hesitation. "I think of Dale because that

Waltrip is one of nine drivers whose first victory was in the Daytona 500: Waltrip, Tiny Lund, Mario Andretti, Pete Hamilton, Derrike Cope, Sterling Marlin, Trevor Bayne, Michael McDowell, and Austin Cindric.

The Waltrips are among nine sets of brothers with Cup Series victories: the Waltrips, the Labontes, the Burtons, the Allisons, the Flocks, the Thomases, the Busches, the Parsonses, and the Bodines.

loss was way bigger than my win. I'm a Christian guy. I believe we're going to heaven, and I believe that when Dale Jr. and I drove off from Turn Four [running one-two and content to finish one-two], I think Dale had a smile on his face. I don't know how many people can say that. Usually when you go, it's not good. But when he went, it was really good. He was a believer, which means he saw his son and his friend going to win the Daytona 500. He was in heaven within the blink of an eye."

As for the time immediately after the accident: "It's thirty or forty minutes later and you still haven't seen your buddy, the guy who was a big reason you won," Waltrip said. "You've started asking questions and wondering. And then the news comes that Dale has died. I don't know how else to sum it up. It went from the best day to the worst. People call it a bittersweet race, but I don't remember the sweet part. When you sum it all up, it was just a hard day."

Consider all that had gone before:

Waltrip, twenty-two at the time, followed his brother, Darrell, into Cup in 1985. He was glib and articulate, an ofttime goofy, fun-loving extrovert much like ol' DW. The problem was, he lacked ol' DW's driving gene. When Darrell said he was too busy to help him get started, Michael began the journey on his own. He moved from Kentucky to North Carolina and lived with Richard Petty, who suggested he skip Xfinity and go directly to Cup. After four good seasons in the Darlington Dash / Baby Grand Series for subcompact cars, he took Petty's advice.

Waltrip won races and a championship in that feeder series. That was good enough to earn a Cup ride with Chuck Rider. They stayed together 1986–1995 before Waltrip spent 1996–1998 with Wood Brothers Racing, 1999 with Jim Mattei, and 2000 with Jim Smith. He landed his dream job in 2001, signing on with DEI. That year's Daytona 500 was his first start with teammates Earnhardt Jr. and Park. As usual for the previous eighteen years, Earnhardt Sr. was driving the No. 3 Chevrolet for Richard Childress Racing.

Despite losing its heart and soul in the 500, DEI kept racing through 2008. It used fifteen drivers in those thirteen seasons, four of them combining for twenty-four victories. (In 2001, Earnhardt Jr., Park, and Waltrip combined for five victories.) Earnhardt Jr. had seventeen of DEI's twenty-four victories, Waltrip had four, Park had two, and Martin Truex Jr. one.

Waltrip left DEI after the 2005 season. By then, Park was out of racing because of a head injury and Earnhardt Jr. was driving for Hendrick Motorsports. Waltrip drove one year for Doug Bawel, then fielded his own mid-pack team for eight years. He made a handful of ceremonial starts from 2010 through 2016 before retiring in 2017 at age fifty-four.

Today, he remains the "Mikey" whose first Cup Series victory was his best *and* his worst.

CHAPTER 47

Rusty Wallace

Bristol (TN) Motor Speedway, Apr. 6, 1986

R usty Wallace made a rather startling debut in the NASCAR Cup Series.

In the very first race of his Cup career, Wallace stunned much of the garage area and much of NASCAR's fan base by finishing second. He drove a Roger Penske–owned Chevrolet in the 1980 spring race at Atlanta, finishing nine and one-half seconds behind the winning driver, another up-and-comer named Dale Earnhardt.

Wallace, a native of St. Louis, had burned up the short tracks of the Midwest and labeled himself ready to try the big time. Don Miller, a long-time associate of Penske, a motorsports kingpin, was a Wallace friend and advocate. He worked out the deal that put Wallace, who once had been Miller's newspaper delivery boy, in the Penske car at Atlanta.

If it was a test of sorts, Wallace got an A-plus.

"We bugged Roger about running the car at Atlanta," Miller said. "He really didn't want us to mess with it, but he said, 'Just go ahead. If you want to put that car together, you do it on your own time.' We worked on it at night in the shop. We finally put the deal together on a handshake at a Christmas party in 1979."

A key rival of
Dale Earnhardt,
Rusty Wallace
turned short-track
success into Cup
Series wins and a
championship.
*BARB SAUNDERS /
BRH RACING ARCHIVES*

The patched-together team showed up in Atlanta simply hoping to qualify for the race and to give Wallace a little experience at a fast superspeedway. "It wasn't that I didn't think he had the talent because I believed he did," Miller said. "I guess the key thing was he had no experience. It was his very first one. As it turned out, he ran like a house afire in that old Caprice."

It was rather telling that Earnhardt and Wallace finished one-two in Rusty's debut. They would become very good friends and very competitive rivals over the decades to come—a relationship of equal parts ferocity and respect.

But first, Wallace had to show he was one position better than Atlanta. Despite his fine run in that first race, it was six more years before he crossed the finish line first, that breakthrough moment coming in the Valleydale 500 April 6, 1986, at Bristol, Tennessee.

Wallace's acceleration took some time because it took him years to put together a full-time, first-class program. He ran only nine Cup races between 1980 and 1983 before finally nailing a full-time ride with team owner Cliff Stewart in 1984. He joined champion drag racer Raymond Beadle's NASCAR team in 1986, setting up the first of fifty-five career Cup victories and paving the road to a championship.

On a cloudy race day at Bristol, a track where he ultimately would score nine victories (his personal record at a speedway), Wallace dominated the second half of the 500, handing Pontiac its first series win in almost two years. Twelve of the thirty-two starters failed to finish.

Wallace coasted at the end, outrunning second-place Ricky Rudd by 10.69 seconds. He led the final 101 laps.

"I can't say a word," said Wallace, who proceeded to say many more. "It was great—the dream of a lifetime. I didn't think it would ever happen. I worked so hard, so hard. The last thirty laps seemed like two hundred. I just kept driving every line as careful as I could."

Crew chief Barry Dodson said the win was proof of what was to come.

Rusty Wallace was a participant in one of the most controversial finishes in the history of NASCAR's All-Star race. In the 1989 version, then called the Winston, Wallace, running second, shoved Darrell Waltrip out of the lead and won the race, leading an angry Waltrip to say he hoped Wallace choked on his winnings.

"Some people doubted Rusty's ability, but anyone who has won two hundred short-track races is a winner," Dodson said. "Some people doubted he'd ever make it big. Well, he made it big today. Mark this date."

There would be many other victory-lane dates for Wallace.

In 1989, he won six times, scored thirteen top fives, and won the Cup championship in Beadle's cars. It would be his only Cup title.

Four years later, having moved on to Roger Penske's team and one of the most successful partnerships in NASCAR history, Wallace stormed to ten victories, although he finished second in points to Earnhardt, who won six times.

That season was yet another year that Wallace and Earnhardt fought for the sport's high ground.

"They were friends off the race track, but once they got on the race track it was Katy bar the door," said Miller, who was along for much of the ride with Wallace. "I was spotting for Rusty in a race at Wilkesboro, and he and Earnhardt were going at it. I said, 'Rusty, cool it. Let him go right now. We can't win halfway through the race.' They were beating and banging on each other. I said, 'You're going to wreck the car.' He said, 'I'm selling T-shirts.'"

Miller was not present for Wallace's breakthrough Cup win.

Despite totaling fifty-five Cup victories and winning at least one race in seventeen of his twenty-six years at NASCAR's top level, Wallace failed to win a race at Daytona International Speedway and Talladega Superspeedway, traditionally the sport's fastest tracks.

"I was listening to it on the radio with a bunch of friends in St. Louis," he said. "I talked to him on the phone afterward. I said, 'That was really a cool win.' He said, 'Yeah, and I think we can do it again next week.'

"You could see all that in him when he was young. He had a fire burning in his belly. He was going to do something. And he did it. He worked his guts out building [short-track] cars for other people so he could have enough money to race his own."

CHAPTER 48

Dale Jarrett

Michigan International Speedway, Aug. 18, 1991

There are moments when former NASCAR Cup Series champion Dale Jarrett wonders what might have been. What if he'd poured all his time, energy, and athleticism into golf? What if he'd accepted that golf scholarship from the University of South Carolina? And what if a touring pro had seen enough potential to suggest that Jarrett should apply to the PGA's Q-School in hopes of getting a Tour card?

And what if he hadn't been so smitten by one lower-series race at Hickory Speedway that he'd choose his life's path right then and there?

If Jarrett's life had taken even one turn, he might have become famous at Augusta National, Pebble Beach, and Muirfield Village instead of Daytona Beach, Charlotte, and Indianapolis. His rivals would have been Phil Mickelson, Tiger Woods, and Greg Norman instead of Dale Earnhardt, Bill Elliott, and Jeff Gordon.

That's because he was good enough at golf to attract attention from the University of South Carolina. The offer was tempting until Jarrett realized he'd rather play golf without the burden of having to go to class. The decision to turn down South Carolina came with second thoughts; who knows what might have been?

Dale Jarrett
followed his father,
Ned, into NASCAR
and later joined him
in the Hall of Fame.
DICK CONWAY

"The thing was, I was a competitor in everything," the sixty-four-year-old Jarrett explained. "I played everything in high school: football, basketball, baseball, golf. I loved to compete. My high school grades were good enough to get by, but the truth is that I was in school mainly to play sports. The thought of going to class after high school didn't appeal to me."

Early on, Jarrett was drawn more to golf than racing. He was mostly self-taught, with help from his father, Ned, a fifty-time race winner, Hall of Famer, and two-time Cup champion. Dale's first sub-par round (two-under-seventy) came at age fifteen at Glen Oaks Country Club in Maiden, North Carolina. He eventually reached a one-handicap and won the 1975 Glen Oaks championship as a teenager. Would that have gotten him to the PGA's Qualifying School?

"That's a possibility, but I don't know if I would ever have gotten to that level," he admits. "I've played with pros on good courses, and I doubt I would have reached their level. I've seen how good they are, how they do things that ninety-nine percent of us can't do. Golf is a very hard game to master. I don't think I would have succeeded in golf like in racing."

Speaking of which . . .

His debut was a twenty-five-lap Limited Sportsman feature at Hickory in 1977. He started last and finished ninth and quickly realized he'd found his calling. "I told Dad, 'I don't know how I'm going to do this, but this is exactly what I've been looking for,'" Jarrett said many years later. "That was after one twenty-five-lap race. I'd done everything in high school sports, but nothing felt as good as driving that car. It was the most exhilarating thing I'd ever done."

Jarrett is among the seven second-generation drivers with Cup victories. The others: Richard Petty, Buddy Baker, Kyle Petty, Davey Allison, Dale Earnhardt Jr., and Chase Elliott.

Between then and 1981, Jarrett advanced from weekly tracks to the Xfinity Series. By 1984, he was in Cup with a handful of well-intended but underfunded owners. Later, he drove with success for owners Cale Yarborough, the Wood Brothers, Joe Gibbs, Robert Yates, and Michael Waltrip. His resume is impressive: eleven Xfinity victories; thirty-two Cup victories; the 1999 Cup Series title with Robert Yates Racing; four victories each at Michigan and Daytona Beach (including three Daytona 500s); three victories each at Charlotte, Darlington, and Pocono; two Brickyard 400s; and thirteen combined victories at eleven other venues. In 2014, he was inducted into the NASCAR Hall of Fame.

The first of those thirty-two Cup victories came in August 1991 with the Wood Brothers at Michigan International Speedway. Jarrett had gotten the coveted No. 21 Ford ride in April 1990 when Neil Bonnett was sidelined by a crash at Darlington, South Carolina. Ned had often reminded team co-owner Eddie Wood to keep Dale in mind if he ever needed a driver. When Bonnett was hurt, the Woods quickly made the call.

"At first we thought we'd only need Dale for the next weekend at Bristol," Wood explained. "Then, on Monday, we learned that Neil couldn't run Bristol. In fact, they didn't know how long he'd be out. That's how we got Dale, but we didn't know for how long. We had him most of 1990 and all of 1991 before he went to Gibbs, where his brother-in-law [Jimmy Makar] was building that new company."

In their forty-second race together, in August of 1991, Jarrett and the Woods started eleventh in the Champion Spark Plug 400 at MIS. Jarrett led one lap near halfway, then led eleven of the last twelve to beat Davey Allison by about eight inches. A gamble on a late-race, gas-only pit stop put Jarrett in a position to challenge Allison, who led a race-high sixty-one laps. In the TV booth, Ned was understandably overcome with emotion as his son joined the list of Cup Series winners.

"From where I was watching in our pit box, I knew Dale had won," Wood said. "He got by Davey at the very last split second, and I could tell he had won. But I didn't go nuts and jump up and down until the NASCAR radio said 'twenty-one–twenty-eight.'"

Today, more than thirty years later, Jarrett still cherishes that moment. "It was everything I'd hoped for and more," he said of his first victory. "My first thought wasn't that I'd won for me; I'd won for the Woods. That made the moment even more special because our families have been friends for years. My dad and Glen and Leonard [Wood] went back so far. That family gave me a second chance and put me in position to stay in Cup. They gave me the ride that kept my career going."

After sixteen more years and thirty-one more victories with various owners, Jarrett retired in 2008 after two disappointing seasons with Michael Waltrip Racing. And why not? After all, he was fifty-one and "fun golf" was calling again.

CHAPTER 49

Brad Keselowski

Talladega (AL) Superspeedway, Apr. 26, 2009

F ew drivers have made their first entrance into a NASCAR Cup
victory lane accompanied by as many fireworks as Brad Keselowski.

It happened April 26, 2009, on an otherwise normal day at Talladega
Superspeedway. Of course, "normal" at Talladega is not the same normal
as at most tracks. As expected in virtually every race at the oversized
superspeedway, there were huge multicar wrecks, tight drafting, and
risky moves at 200-mile-per-hour-plus speeds.

The difference, however, came at the end.

With one lap to go, Carl Edwards and Keselowski, drafting together
in a tight tandem, flew past the lead duo of Ryan Newman and Dale
Earnhardt Jr. This put Edwards in the lead, with Keselowski shadowing
his bumper as they roared through Turns One and Two for the last time.
Entering the final two miles of the race, Keselowski, racing part-time in
Cup that season, saw his chance, and he didn't hesitate.

As Keselowski and Edwards approached the checkered flag, Keselowski
moved up the track to the outside. Edwards moved up to block. Then
Keselowski dropped low to attempt to pass on the inside. Edwards tried
to block that move, too, but Keselowski was having none of it. He kept his

Brad Keselowski's first victory came in a wild finish at Talladega Superspeedway. *NIGEL KINRADE*

foot in the throttle and hit Edwards. Edwards's car went into a slide and then into the air.

The next few seconds were perhaps the most breathtaking of that season.

Edwards's car sailed into the fencing along the frontstretch, sending parts and pieces into the grandstand and injuring several fans. Then his car, which also was hit by Newman's, stopped on the track, the engine compartment in flames.

Meanwhile, Keselowski was crossing the finish line, the first win of his career notched. The last lap was the only lap he led all day, and, in fact, was the first Cup lap he had ever led.

Edwards, who wasn't injured despite the dramatic nature of the crash, climbed from his car and ran on foot to the finish line, "completing" the race (although, obviously, he wasn't given credit for the lap because he didn't have the car with him).

It was a crazy day at a place that has seen more than its share of crazy days.

"Coming off Turn Two, I knew I had a move, but I didn't know what I was going to have to do," Keselowski remembered years later. "If I moved high, he [Edwards] would cover it, and that would give me an opening inside. I never thought there would be a wreck like that."

Keselowski finished the race having pushed his Chevrolet to the limit. "Every gauge on my dash was glowing red," he said. "The temp and the RPMs were high. I just knew it was going to blow up at any moment.

"When it got to the end, I had no option. When he [Edwards] went high and then came back down, there was no way to avoid contact without going below the yellow line, which would have meant losing the race. I wasn't going to do that."

And, he understated, "The results aren't always pretty."

The raucous victory lane celebration was just the beginning of the fun. Keselowski drove for Florida car owner James Finch, a construction company owner who raced part-time in the Cup Series for twenty years. The win was the first—and last—of Finch's ownership career, and he was known as someone who enjoyed the occasional party.

"Oh, we had several parties," Keselowski said. "We made the most of that win, without a doubt.

"I left the track feeling kind of surreal. Did this really happen? It was like living a dream."

The trophy—and the winning car—are on display in Keselowski's race shop.

The Talladega win was really only the start of the dream for Keselowski, the star of a Michigan racing family and a smart driver who had been tabbed as someone to watch on the big stage. The win (and his aggressive driving) played a role in earning Keselowski a seat with Penske Racing with three races remaining in the 2009 season, and he was off on a charmed ride with one of motorsports' top operations.

Keselowski won three Cup races in 2011 and increased that total to five in 2012, a year that also saw him win the

Keselowski's NASCAR career received a significant boost when he joined Dale Earnhardt Jr.'s Nationwide Series team in 2007. He won races at Nashville and Bristol in 2008.

> Late in 2007, a few months after moving from Michigan
> to North Carolina to enhance his chances at NASCAR
> success, Keselowski suffered a bad case of influenza.
> Willie Jackson, husband of Dale Earnhardt Jr.'s mother,
> Brenda Jackson, discovered Keselowski in dire straits at
> his townhouse and rushed him to a doctor. Keselowski
> stayed with the Jacksons for several days as he
> recovered.

Cup championship. He would stay with Penske through the 2021 season, scoring at least one win every year before moving into a team ownership role with veteran owner Jack Roush.

Keselowski sometimes drew criticism in the early years of his career for overly aggressive driving, and he found himself in feuds with several drivers, but he was rarely apologetic.

"It's not possible to get a Cup ride right now without being aggressive and without having some swagger in your step," he said after joining Penske Racing. "Does that make you a jerk? To some people, yes. To some people, no. It depends on where you're coming from. If you look at the sport right now, there are no new drivers coming in.

"So whatever I'm doing is working, and it's gotten me to where I'm at, and I've survived this [lack] of development drivers that are not getting opportunities because of that attitude, because of that aggressiveness."

CHAPTER 50

Denny Hamlin

Pocono (PA) Raceway, June 11, 2006

It was a bitterly cold Saturday in December of 2003 when Denny Hamlin's life changed in ways he might never have expected. Even today—almost nineteen years later—he remembers the moment as if it were yesterday.

Hamlin was a twenty-three-year-old Late Model driver, talented and ambitious enough to someday be at NASCAR's upper level. He had spent most of his teen years racing Mini-Stock, Legend, and Late Models on weekend short tracks in the Carolinas and Virginia. Like so many teenage racers with talent but meager resources, he needed something to get his career started up the ladder.

Enter retired NASCAR driver Curtis Markham, a member of Joe Gibbs Racing's (JGR's) driver development program. Among his tasks was to find young drivers skilled enough to join JGR, then mentor them through the lower ranks and toward the Cup Series. As such, Markham arranged an on-track audition at Hickory Motor Speedway shortly after the 2003 season.

If not for that chilly 2003 audition, Hamlin likely wouldn't be among NASCAR's brightest stars entering his eighteenth season with JGR in the No. 11 FedEx Toyota. He probably wouldn't have forty-six

Denny Hamlin became a star for Joe Gibbs Racing after winning for the first time at Pocono Raceway in 2006. *DAVID GRIFFIN*

Cup victories, including three Daytona 500s and two Southern 500s. He probably wouldn't have been 2006 Rookie of the Year or enjoyed thirteen top-ten points seasons. Almost assuredly, Hamlin wouldn't be a cinch for the NASCAR Hall of Fame when he becomes eligible upon retirement in a few years.

This is how Markham played such a crucial role in helping Hamlin get the first of his forty-six Cup victories at Pocono (Pennsylvania) Raceway in June of 2006:

Throughout the late 1990s and early 2000s, Hamlin was a promising young star on the weekend short tracks in the Southeast. As a teenager, he came through Mini-Stocks into Late Models, determined to eventually reach the Cup Series. Despite his talent—he was a consistent winner throughout his career—he faced the familiar challenge of finding an owner willing to give him a chance. His family-owned team had done all it could, but by the early 2000s its racing budget was beginning to feel the strain.

Markham and Hamlin were twenty-one years apart, but knew each other since they were well-known racers from the Richmond area. It happened that when Markham was planning his "gong show" audition, Hamlin was looking to sell a handful of race-ready Late Models. Markham asked him to bring them to Hickory, prepare them for the test, help evaluate the candidates, then make the cars available for sale later that afternoon.

But a funny thing happened in the early stages of the test.

"Denny took his car out and ran some laps, and I was watching him," Markham said years later. "I couldn't believe what I was seeing. "I said to [JGR associate] Steve de Souza, 'He's got great car control.' Denny was as good as anything I'd seen in a young driver in quite a while. I called [the late] J. D. Gibbs back at the race shop and told him we had who we needed, that we didn't need to look at anybody else. I stayed on him about Denny until they finally signed him up. The rest is history."

With forty-six victories, Hamlin is the second-winningest Cup Series driver without a championship. Junior Johnson won fifty races but never won a title. Mark Martin retired with forty victories and no championships.

And what a history it's been.

After a handful of promising Camping World and Xfinity starts in 2004, the organization gave Hamlin a few Cup starts and the full Xfinity schedule in 2005. He ran a few Xfinity races and the full Cup schedule in 2006, joining Tony Stewart and J. J. Yeley in the lineup. He responded by going pole-to-victory twice at Pocono Raceway and finishing third in points that year, making 2006 Rookie of the Year something of a runaway.

Over the next sixteen seasons, Hamlin added forty-four more Cup victories to his resume. He's won at least once annually for fifteen of his sixteen full seasons, missing only in 2018. His career highs are eight victories in 2010 and seven victories in 2020. His Daytona 500 victories were 2016, 2019, and 2020; his Southern 500 victories in 2017 and 2021; and he won the 2015 NASCAR All-Star race. All told, he's won at eighteen of NASCAR's twenty-five active tracks.

"There's no question I wouldn't be here if it hadn't been for Curtis that day at Hickory," Hamlin said last year prior to the NASCAR Awards Banquet in Nashville. "He's the one who made that crucial call back to the shop and told J. D. they needed to hire me. He said, 'We might not be looking *for* him, but we need to look *at* him.' He knew my short-track background from racing against me and from people we both knew back home.

"I was so motivated to show off in front of the Gibbs employees that Saturday at Hickory. I wanted to give my best, and I think I did. They were wowed. Even if I hadn't been good enough, I think Curtis had a warm place in his heart for me because he knew my short-track history back in Virginia. I think he was going to pump me up to the Gibbs people. But, in either case, I think I was clearly the best one there that day."

It didn't take long for Hamlin to show Markham and the Gibbs people they were right. Twenty-one races into his Cup career, he started on the pole and led six times for 83 of the 200 laps to win the June 2006 Pocono 500. He did it again less than a month later, leading 151 of 200 laps in the Pennsylvania 500.

Among Hamlin's prized possessions is a photo of him as an eleven-year-old meeting Joe Gibbs, then coach of the Washington Football Team, early in the 1990s. Both men confirm that Hamlin brazenly said he'd one day drive for Gibbs's new NASCAR team.

"The car was so good that first Pocono race that I knew we had a good chance," Hamlin recalled. "I was so nervous because I knew we had the best car there. It was a matter of saying to myself, 'How can I not screw this up?' We cut a tire about midway [forcing an unscheduled green-flag stop], but the car was so good I was able to come back. All the stars aligned just right that day. It was such a special win."

ACKNOWLEDGMENTS

Chasing stock car racers across the continent—and occasionally across the Big Pond—isn't a task for those without a big suitcase. The travel is often long and sometimes difficult (try a blizzard in Atlanta on race weekend in an eventful March). The stories are sometimes painfully hard to write. Writers who cover most other sports generally aren't confronted with reporting about sudden death, in particular the passing of a beloved superstar.

Being on the NASCAR watch for decades means riding along on a circus train full of unusual individuals, from drivers to mechanics to wealthy team owners to down-on-their-luck independent racers to the rafts of suits who run the show, for better or worse.

We have seen the best and worst of this traveling menagerie, and many of the stories that have crossed our paths appear in this book, the contents of which serve as a sort of survey of NASCAR's sometimes ragged and rough history.

Many people shared the ride.

First, our love and gratitude to two long-suffering wives—Francie Pearce and Polly Hembree—who put up with the unending travel and the phone calls interrupting dinner and sleep and kids' piano concerts. And the unfortunate calls from a racetrack phone announcing a rainout and, yes, another day at the track.

Our thanks to hundreds of media colleagues who shared press boxes and media centers and garage areas across the years. Far too many to list here, but advice and examples from some of the pioneer writers in auto racing were very helpful. Despite the dramatic changes in the media landscape over the years, including the loss of many fine reporters to the contraction of journalism, media centers remain a place of camaraderie and good humor.

Thanks, also, to the many public relations representatives and track and team officials who have worked in the sport over the years. And also to our editors at *Autoweek*, long a bastion of quality motorsports journalism.

Thank you to eagle-eye editor Jim McLaurin, a motorsports media center stalwart, and to the photographers whose work brightens these pages.

Our appreciation, too, to the drivers who sat for interviews and to those we had to chase across garage areas for post-race comments. Sometimes, that was the race after the race.

It's been a trip.

BIBLIOGRAPHY

Edelstein, Robert. *NASCAR Legends: Memorable Men, Moments, and Machines in Racing History.* New York: Overlook Press, 2011.

Fielden, Greg. *Forty Years of Stock Car Racing,* 5 vols. Surfside Beach, SC: Galfield Press, 1987.

Fielden, Larry. *Tim Flock: Race Driver.* Surfside Beach, SC: Galfield Press, 1991.

Hunter, Jim. *21 Forever: The Story of Stock Car Driver David Pearson.* Huntsville, AL: Strode Publishers, 1980.

Kelly, Godwin. *Fireball: Legends Don't Fall from the Sky.* Daytona Beach, FL: Carbon Press, 2005.

Zeller, Bob. *Daytona 500: An Official History.* Phoenix: David Bull Publishing, 2002.

INDEX

Al Pearce saw his first NASCAR race in 1966 in Daytona Beach, Florida. The first race he covered was in July of 1969 at Dover, Delaware, for *The Times-Herald* of Newport News, Virginia. Since then, he's covered thousands of races of all types—NASCAR, IndyCar, Formula One, NHRA and IHRA drag racing, APBA powerboats, SCCA, international sports cars and weekly short-track races for *Tribune Co.* (1969–2004) and *Autoweek* magazine (1973–current).

Pearce has authored thirteen books on racing and has covered events throughout the US and five foreign countries. He is an eight-time Virginia sports writing award winner and the recipient of a half dozen national and regional sports halls of fame awards. He currently lives in Newport News, Virginia, with his wife, Francie.

Mike Hembree has written about auto racing for four decades and is the author of fourteen books, including seven racing titles. He has won numerous awards, including the American Motorsports Media Award of Excellence. He also is a seven-time National Motorsports Press Association Writer of the Year and a three-time winner of the Russ Catlin Award for motorsports journalism excellence. Hembree has covered auto racing for *Autoweek*, *USA Today*, the *Greenville News* (SC), the *Spartanburg Herald-Journal* (SC), the *SPEED Channel* and *NASCAR Scene*. His newspaper career also includes coverage of the NFL, the NBA, Major League Baseball, the Olympics, and golf. He is a graduate of the University of South Carolina with a BA in Journalism, and he currently lives in Gaffney, South Carolina, with his wife, Polly.

OTHER BOOKS BY AL PEARCE
Holman–Moody: The Legendary Race Team
The Unauthorized NASCAR Fan Guide
Dale Earnhardt Jr.: Inside the Rise of a NASCAR Superstar
The Illustrated History of Stock Car Racing
Stock Car Racing Chronicle: The 1990s
Famous Tracks

OTHER BOOKS BY MIKE HEMBREE
NASCAR: The Definitive History of America's Sport
Dale Earnhardt Jr.: Out of the Shadow of Greatness
100 Things NASCAR Fans Should Know and Do before They Die
Taking Stock: Life in NASCAR's Fast Lane
"Then Tony Said to Junior . . ."

CPSIA information can be obtained
at www.ICGtesting.com
Printed in the USA
LVHW050159241122
733963LV00006B/145